Dolls' House Accessories, Fixtures and Fittings

Dolls' House Accessories, Fixtures and Fittings

ANDREA BARHAM

Guild of Master Craftsman Publications Ltd

First published 1998 by

Reprinted 2001, 2004

Guild of Master Craftsman Publications Ltd,
166 High Street, Lewes,
East Sussex BN7 1XU

© Andrea Barham 1998

ISBN 1 86108 103 0

Photographs by Andrew Barham

Line drawings by David Crawley

Designed by Angela Neal
Typeface: Bembo
Colour origination by Viscan Graphics (Singapore)
Printed and bound by Kyodo Singapore

To Mum and Dad for your unstinting encouragement and support. (And for giving me my first dolls' house.)

CONTENTS

ACKNOWLEDGEMENTS

I am indebted to my husband Andy for his photographic skills and his patience;
to my father David for drawing the patterns and templates; to my editor Lindy Dunlop
for her invaluable input and to Liz Inman from whose original commission this book grew.

NOTE ON MEASUREMENTS

Throughout the book measurements have been given in imperial and metric,
with the converted measurements given in brackets. For each project,
use one system consistently as the conversions are not exact.

Introduction

Dolls' house collecting and miniature modelling are popular adult hobbies. Well-heeled collectors spend thousands of pounds furnishing miniature mansions, but you don't have to spend a small fortune on your dolls' house. Enthusiasts can make a surprising array of accessories and furnishings themselves. This is very satisfying, not to mention cost-effective, and your house will then be a unique heirloom. No special skills are needed to make miniature accessories – just a little patience and know-how.

Miniature modelling is a quirky hobby (who else would have one 'large cherub' on her shopping list?), but in many ways it is the perfect one because it combines the thrill of collecting with the satisfaction of crafting. Gone are the days when miniaturists were obliged to make most things themselves. Nowadays practically anything can be bought or commissioned. I hope this doesn't deter the DIY enthusiast because there's no substitute for exercising your own creativity and self-expression.

Although I have made a huge variety of miniatures over many years, I am not an expert in any field of craft or woodwork – but I'll have a go at anything! Great things have been achieved by people who didn't know their limitations. This book gives a taste of the different media, skills and crafts the enthusiastic miniaturist can adapt and will guide recent converts through making their first simple miniatures. The projects show just a few examples of what you can make using various techniques and media. If you take to miniature marquetry or cross stitch, why not find out more about the craft? Have a go at everything and you'll soon find where your natural skills lie.

The following projects are in the traditional scale of an inch to a foot (1/12 scale). Most of the techniques can be adapted to a smaller scale. I have concentrated on larger pieces in this book, but many of the techniques can be used to make tiny accessories. Read through the entire project first and collect the necessary materials before beginning work. If it doesn't come right the first time, have another go – this is the best way to learn. Your miniatures will soon be the envy of your friends.

CHAPTER ONE

Materials and Equipment

Materials and Equipment

No elaborate or expensive tools are needed to make miniature dolls' house accessories

and furnishings. If you have dabbled in DIY you probably have most of the tools required.

It is worth investing in some paints and specialist preparations. Once you have them,

all manner of miniature possibilities unfold. It's also useful to have a workstation in

which to keep the tools and finishes you use most often. A fishing tackle box is ideal.

TOOLS

The following tools will get you off to a good start.

Small, thin-nosed pliers These are indispensable for shaping and bending. It's useful if they also cut wire.

Junior hacksaw Be sure to fit the blade correctly when you change it. The cutting edge should bite on the forward stroke.

Mitre block A must for cutting accurate mitres (the joints in moulding such as skirting).

Power scissors Every miniaturist should have a pair. They look like regular scissors with a serrated blade and can be used to cut through thin metal, wood and plastic.

Manicure scissors Useful for fiddly cutting.

Craft knife The type with changeable blades are the most economical.

Sandpaper Only use fine grades and always sand along the grain.

Hand or mini power drill with tiny drill bits The most useful sizes are ⅛in, ⅟₁₆in and ⅟₃₂in.

Mini power tools These can be useful to the enthusiastic DIY miniaturist because they speed up a project. A mini power drill has a variety of uses. It can drill, sand, rout (gouge) and grind. A

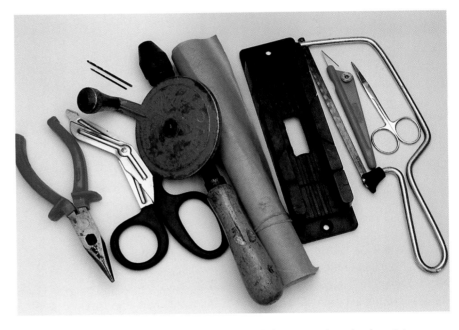

Fig 1.1 A few basic tools. From left to right: small thin-nosed pliers, power scissors, hand or mini power drill, sandpaper, mitre block, junior hacksaw, craft knife, manicure scissors.

mini jigsaw is only useful if you intend to construct furniture from scratch. I have never felt the need to invest in a lathe since turned hardware, such as banister spindles, is cheap and readily available.

Old leather gloves Last but not least. I wear these when I'm sanding, staining, cutting or sawing. The gloves have a few cuts in them but at least my fingers are all still attached!

ADHESIVES

There is a bewildering range of adhesives on the market, but I get along with just four: PVA glue (tacky glue), epoxy resin (Araldite), cyanoacrylic glue (superglue) and wood glue.

Polyvinyl acetate (PVA) glue Also known as white craft glue, tacky glue, R/C Modeller's Glue and Aleene's

Tacky Glue. A readily-available craft glue, it is thick, white, water soluble and usually comes in a squeezy bottle. A great all-purpose glue for dolls' house crafters, it is quick drying and dries clear. PVA glue will glue wood faster than wood glue, but the joint will remain flexible. Wood glue is best for a rigid joint, as when gluing a picture frame.

Epoxy resin The best-known epoxy resin is Araldite. It comes in two tubes. Mix equal quantities of adhesive and hardener together to activate the clear adhesive. This may seem inconvenient, but the bond is as strong as you'll find. It doesn't cure instantly, but the rapid setting brands cure in just a few minutes.

Mixing may become tedious during a project with several gluing stages. To speed things along, squeeze a line of adhesive next to a line of hardener. Mix a little together from the top of the lines with a cocktail stick. When this hardens, mix up a little more. If you want a longer curing time, mix in a little less hardener.

Never muddle the lids. If the hardener in the lid cures the adhesive in the tube, you will never get the lid off again!

Cyanoacrylic glue Universally known as superglue. There are several brands on the market, but all contain the same active ingredient and come in tubes or bottles. (Tubes tend to leak which results in gluey fingers.) The gel formula is the easiest to control. There's no need to buy superglue solvent; acetone or nail polish remover will do the trick.

Wood glue A specialist wood adhesive. Once dry it gives a strong inflexible bond – but it does take about half an hour to dry. During this time the bond must be clamped or supported. Wood can also be successfully glued with Araldite which dries faster.

Glass glue Another specialist glue which will glue glass to glass or glass to

Fig 1.2 The four most useful forms of glue for making miniatures.

metal. It is very similar to superglue, but cures only in ultraviolet light. (For more information on how to use glass glue, see Chapter 12, pages 134–136.)

Balsa cement A stringy, clear adhesive. This is occasionally useful for providing a semi-permanent bond. Balsa cement sticks adequately, but the bond can be snapped apart. Why is this useful? I use it for gluing exterior and interior trim such as door surrounds. This means that they can be easily prised off if I decide to redecorate. Wood glue bonds so strongly that prising trim off would damage the wall or the trim or both.

PAINTS

When decorating a dolls' house, inside or out, one of the easiest finishes is paint. There are three types of paint – water-based (e.g. acrylic model paint), solvent-based (e.g. oil paint) and cellulose-based (e.g. car spray paint). Household emulsion paint can also be used to good effect. If it's too thick, it can be thinned with a little water. Emulsion tends to come in a paler colour range than hobby paint.

Household gloss and matt solvent-

WATER-BASED PAINTS

◆ You may need to apply several coats of a water-based paint to get good coverage.

◆ Both matt and gloss finishes are available in acrylic and emulsion paints.

◆ There is an excellent range of shades, but if you can't find the right one, colours can be mixed.

◆ Mix plenty of paint so you don't run out halfway through a project and have to re-blend the colour.

◆ If you blend a shade for decorating, store some in a plastic film capsule, in case you need to retouch.

◆ Never mix solvent-based paints with water-based acrylics: the pigments are dissolved in different solutions and won't combine.

◆ Always use the appropriate solvent to dilute paint that has become too thick. Use water (or proprietary acrylic solvent) to dilute water-based paints and solvent such as white spirit to dilute solvent-based paints.

Fig 1.3 Some useful types of paint: cellulose, water-based and solvent-based.

based paint (woodwork paint) can be used in the same way as solvent-based model paint.

If you can't find the shade you want, mix the colours, but always mix like with like. (You can sometimes get away with mixing acrylic and emulsion as they are both water based.)

It is generally wise to undercoat everything you intend to paint. An undercoat will give a smooth, hard-wearing surface to paint on. Don't forget, if you're new to the hobby you

only need five basic colours to begin with: yellow, blue, red, black and white.

Water-based paints

Modern water-based emulsions and acrylics are very easy to work with and all you need for decorating a dolls' house inside and out. It is not necessary to buy specialist brands: the standard emulsions and acrylics you have around the house will do just as good a job. Sample pots of emulsion are available from DIY stores in an ever-changing variety of colours.

Water-based paints, such as emulsion or acrylic paint, are best for interior walls, ceilings, 'plaster' such as cornices and 'woodwork' such as skirting. Their great advantage is that they are very easy to work with and very easy to clean: the brushes wash out in water. Sample pots of emulsion are ideal. You can also use proprietary pots of acrylic model paint. These come in gloss, matt, metallic and satin. They work out more expensive, but the colour range includes deeper shades which can be useful for a period effect.

Solvent-based paints

You can usually identify a solvent-based paint by its odour. The solvent is volatile and evaporates into the air when you remove the lid. Examples of solvent-based paints are oil paints, gloss paints and some glass paints. Gold and silver marker pens are generally solvent based.

Solvent-based paints are also known as enamel or oil paints. They are more hardwearing than water-based paints which makes them most suitable for the exterior of your dolls' house. They also give very good coverage, but take considerably longer to dry, and the brushes must be cleaned in a solvent such as white spirit. The range of solvent-based paints tends to be more limited than water-based. You may need to mix different shades to achieve a particular effect. A 14ml tin of model paint doesn't go very far when you are painting the exterior of a dolls' house, so use a 50ml tin of Humbrol enamel paint. The 50ml tins come in a range of 18 colours. If you want a shade that isn't available, purple for example, mix a 14ml tin of Bright Red into a 50ml tin of French Blue. Speaking of purple, don't be afraid to be bold with colour. Although bright aniline dyes weren't available until the mid 1800s, decorators from past times often favoured deep, rich and bold shades – unlike the muted pastel shades common today.

Household matt 'woodwork paint' looks good as an exterior finish, but matt finishes can be hard to find in solvent-based paints. Gloss, especially a high gloss finish, will show up every lump, bump and flaw in your work. A matt finish is kinder to the amateur. One solution is to apply a final coat of matt varnish over gloss paint. (Matt varnish paints on shiny, but dries to a matt finish.) This will take away that nasty sheen and has the added advantage of protecting the paint finish. If you use water-based paint for your exterior finish, it's a good idea to top coat this with matt varnish for protection.

Cellulose-based paints

Cellulose paint, such as car spray paint, can be used successfully on the dolls' house exterior and interior. Spray painting has the advantage of being quick, and the coverage is also very smooth. There is a wide colour range, but of course you can't mix colours, and they are generally all gloss. Use the appropriate car spray primer to undercoat before spraying. Car spray primer can also be used beneath solvent- and water-based paints.

Other spray paints are available, but they are less economical. (For tips on using spray paint, see Spray Painting in Chapter 5.)

COMPONENTS

I have amassed a useful collection of components and materials ranging from tinsel pipe cleaners to an old kitchen drawer base. (When Andy, my husband, comes across a bottle cap, he automatically hands it to me.) If you don't have something listed, but you have something that will do – use that. Invention is part of the fun.

The following sources are a good starting point for collecting assorted components.

Fig 1.4 Haberdashery, fabric, buttons, jewellery findings and catalogue clippings are all useful for making DIY miniatures.

Safety

One pair of eyes and hands must last you a lifetime. When using tools (especially power tools) and chemicals, it pays to take just a few minutes to protect yourself. Over time people can become sensitized to chemicals and develop allergies. This is less likely if you cut down exposure to chemicals.

◆ Avoid inhaling strong-smelling adhesives, paints or chemicals.

◆ Avoid storing chemicals, adhesives and paints under the sink: keep them in the garage, in an outhouse or a shed.

◆ When doing any messy work, get into the habit of wearing disposable plastic gloves to keep adhesives and chemicals off your hands; these can spark off allergies.

◆ Never cut or saw towards yourself.

◆ Never use blunt tools. Sharp tools are safer because no force is required to use them.

◆ Wear plastic safety goggles when using power tools.

General craft catalogues and shops
Discover the world of mail-order craft suppliers in the classified section of craft magazines. Many suppliers have sumptuous mail-order catalogues. *Hobby's Annual* is full of DIY delights for dolls' house enthusiasts. Also keep a lookout for useful bits and bobs in craft and hobby shops.

Specialist miniature suppliers You may need to use a specialist supplier for certain raw materials including fine cane or metal filigrees (see Suppliers, page 146).

Dolls' house magazines Ask your newsagent to order you a dolls' house magazine such as *The Dolls' House Magazine* or *Dolls' House World*. The adverts in these are a mine of valuable information. If a suitable supplier isn't listed, write and ask the editor: they can often put you in touch with a specialist.

Groups and clubs Dolls' house magazines also list local groups and clubs. These can be a great encouragement for beginners. There is even a 'newsletter/digest' group on the Internet called Tiny Talk.

Dolls' house shops Miniaturists are lovely people. Shop owners and suppliers are nearly always enthusiasts and are happy to advise. Some even have web sites on the Internet. Web site addresses are generally given after the postal address.

Charity shops and jumble sales
Here you can often find cheap bits of jewellery, haberdashery and craft components, which can be cannibalized or customized.

CHAPTER TWO

Architectural Features

Architectural Features

Arranging pieces of furniture, however impressive, in a bare room will create a minimalist effect that is not generally popular in dolls' house décor. Why limit the hobby to furnishings and accessories? Not only do architectural features add immeasurably to the overall effect of a room setting, they also give the enthusiast a whole new area to explore. Architectural features lend proportion and add points of interest, all for very little extra expense.

They include chimney breasts, niches, mouldings and plasterwork. A chimney breast can be constructed from a few off-cuts of wood sheet. It will create intriguing corners and cast depth-giving shadows. Trade a little space to create still more interest. A false back wall with a door will give the illusion of a further, inaccessible room. Add a false side wall with a niche cut into it to hold a treasure or a candle.

Miniature architectural mouldings cost a matter of pence per strip yet they give a polished and professional look to a room. Specialists stock every moulding you could possibly require; from cornices and skirting boards to door surrounds and fireplace mouldings. (*See* Suppliers, page 146.) Architectural features can be as simple or as elaborate as your setting and your ambition allows. Have fun with them.

TECHNIQUE

Plaster Casting

Plaster casting involves creating a mould and making casts from it using plaster. Unless you are planning to sell your work, you may think casting several identical items is of limited use, but when you think of the savings to be made by casting all the 'plaster' mouldings for a large house you will see the attraction of casting your own.

For the beginner, the simplest method of casting is to use plaster and a polymer clay such as Fimo. Various types of plaster are available from mail-order suppliers and craft shops. Fine grain 'alabaster' plaster is best for architectural mouldings since it gives the smoothest finish. Any brand is suitable.

The master mould is first cast from an 'original' which can be made from such things as metal, plastic or wood. Any likely-looking bits can be glued together to make the original. If you enjoy casting, you might like to try making your own silicon moulds for two-sided castings with a product such as Silcoform S2.

CEILING ROSE.

PROJECT

Ceiling Rose

For this project I made up an 'original' from a large, decorative metal finding with a button glued to the centre. A master mould could also be made from a single, plastic wardrobe decoration, for example. From it can be made an unlimited number of casts.

Materials

- ◆ Original rose assembly, to cast from
- ◆ Fimo x 1 packet
- ◆ Fine casting plaster
- ◆ Water

METHOD

Making the mould

1 Knead the Fimo block until it is thoroughly softened. (If using oddments, use enough to make up a whole packet.) Form the block into a round shape.

TIP

PLACING THE FIMO BLOCK SOMEWHERE WARM, FOR EXAMPLE, OVER A RADIATOR, WILL CUT DOWN ON THE KNEADING REQUIRED.

2 Rinse and dry the original rose assembly thoroughly and press it evenly into the Fimo block.

3 Carefully catch a corner of the original rose assembly with your fingernail or the edge of a knife. Gently lever it out, taking care not to distort the Fimo mould. If the mould does get a little distorted, place it face down on a flat surface to reshape it. Once the Fimo is cast, the original assembly is no longer needed.

4 Harden the mould for 15 minutes

Fig 2.1 Pressing a cast from an original.

in an oven set on low (100°C/200°F) and allow to cool.

5 Once cool, scrub inside the mould with soap and a nailbrush to remove any traces of loose Fimo.

Casting the rose

1 Mix three heaped teaspoons of plaster with a little cold water to a cream consistency. Stir well to remove all lumps.

2 Dribble the plaster mixture slowly and carefully into the mould to avoid air bubbles. Fill the mould to the top. Holding it on a flat surface, tap the mould firmly several times until no more air bubbles come to the surface.

3 Leave for about 20 minutes or until the plaster is totally hardened.

Fig 2.2 Filling the cast with plaster.

PLASTER CASTING

◆ When selecting the original, bear in mind that the cast will be a slightly smaller, though exact, reproduction. So, the more detail the original has, the more detailed the resulting cast will be.

◆ Any brand of polymer clay can be used to make the mould. I use Fimo. You can use oddments blended together, as the colour of the cast doesn't matter.

◆ Be sure to brush off any fluff or dust from the original as this will spoil the resulting mould.

◆ You can mix water-based paint, such as acrylic or emulsion paint, into plaster to colour it, or paint the casting once it has dried.

◆ Use Polyfilla for a rougher texture – to cast York stone slabs, for example.

◆ Once the casting technique has been learnt, most architectural plaster mouldings with flat backs – such as fire surrounds, niches, brackets and half-columns – can be cast.

◆ Products such as Hobby Time's 'Mouldin' can be used to make two-piece moulds for casting two-sided items such as statues, basins and toilets.

4 Carefully prise the casting out of the mould. Some castings practically fall out; others need some encouragement. If the plaster is stuck to the mould edges, use a craft knife to chip away the excess plaster, then gently lever round the mould with a blunt-ended knife. Once you find a point with some 'give', lever the entire casting out. Don't worry if the back looks messy. This will be sanded before fixing to the ceiling.

5 Tidy the edge of the casting with a craft knife.

6 Sand the back with sandpaper, so that it sits closely against the ceiling.

7 If the ceiling rose is to be fitted

Fig 2.3 Tidying the casting.

with an electrified light, carefully drill a hole through the centre before gluing the rose in place over the corresponding hole in the ceiling.

Fig 2.4 Drilling a hole for the light fitting.

ALTERNATIVE MATERIALS

FOR A MORE STONE-LIKE CAST-ING, SUCH AS A GARDEN STATUE, USE A PLASTER PRODUCT SUCH AS STONECAST WHICH GIVES A HARDER, MORE DURABLE FINISH.

TECHNIQUE

Splatter Painting

All sorts of stone and marble effects can be simulated with paint. Don't feel that these aren't authentic enough for your dolls' house. In previous centuries, well-to-do houses had what was known as 'faux marble'. This was a paint effect created by skilled craftsmen. Paint-effect stone can be used to decorate fire surrounds, skirting boards, columns, busts, washstand tops and bathroom fittings. Use a ready-made fire surround or make up your own using proprietary mouldings (available from Borcraft; see Suppliers, page 146).

Cans of spray paint can be used to achieve an authentically mottled stone effect. Since the object is to create tiny dots and speckles, the technique is very different from the regular spray painting described in Chapter 10. It is easier to do than to explain, so just get stuck in!

Safety

Spray paint (particularly primer) should only be used in well-ventilated areas, ideally outside. If you suffer from a respiratory condition use a face mask that combats vapours.

KNOW-HOW

SPLATTER PAINTING

◆ Experiment with the technique on a piece of scrap card before spraying your furniture.

◆ Press down one side of the spray paint nozzle rather than pressing squarely on top. This should produce a splattery squirt.

◆ Hold the object far enough away that it doesn't catch a full coat of paint, only the speckles.

◆ For even better effect, move the can from side to side as you spray.

◆ Spray painting can create drips which spoil the effect. To prevent this, wipe the nozzle from time to time with kitchen paper.

◆ For very small areas, a splatter paint effect can be achieved by flicking the bristles of a toothbrush loaded with paint.

◆ If you don't like your first attempt, simply respray with primer and have another go!

GRANITE FIRE SURROUND.

FIRE SURROUNDS

- To prevent muddling up your mouldings, mark each moulding with pencil on the back as you unpack them.
- Make the surround at least ½in (13mm) narrower than the chimney breast, if you have one. A chimney breast isn't obligatory; the chimney flue can be on the outside of the house in which case the surround will be fitted flush to the wall.
- The **lintel** is the horizontal section, which goes along the top.
- The **jambs** are the two vertical side pieces. The joints between jambs and lintel aren't usually mitred.
- The **mantel** is the shelf which lies across the lintel. The longer side of the moulding is the top edge.
- Fireplace mantel moulding also makes attractive shelving.
- When fitting fireplaces, ideally they should line up with the chimney.

Fig 2.5 Assembling the basic fire surround.

Granite Fire Surround

Making up your own fire surround from wood mouldings is cheaper than buying ready-made surrounds. The most difficult part is familiarizing yourself with the names the various strips are given. You can design a different surround for each room, ranging from small and simple for the nursery, to large and elaborate for the grander rooms.

METHOD

Making the fire surround

1 Measure the required width and height of the fire surround. My finished surround measured 3⅞ x 5½in (985 x 140mm).

2 Cut and glue three lengths of lintel moulding to make up the plain inner surround. Fireplace lintel moulding is just a plain flat wood strip. If you want to cut your own, the one I used measured ⅛ x ⅝in (3 x 16mm). Make the lintel too tall rather than too short; it can always be trimmed down to size from the base when it's finished.

Materials

- Lintel moulding
- Fireplace surround moulding
- Decorative fireplace surround moulding
- Fireplace mantel moulding
- Wood glue
- Spray paints: white, dull mauve/pink, black and grey primer
- Clear spray lacquer

3 Cut, mitre and glue three lengths of fireplace surround moulding to fit outside the lintel surround. Take care to mitre the correct angles.

4 Cut, glue and mitre three sections of decorative fireplace surround moulding to fit over the base fireplace surround moulding.

5 Cut a length of fireplace mantel to fit along the top of the fireplace

Fig 2.6 Assembling two more decorative surrounds and the mantel shelf.

Fig 2.7 The primed surround.

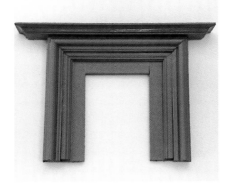

Fig 2.8 The surround sprayed pink.

surround, overlapping the ends. Check you have the mantel the right way up.

6 You can simply stick a length of mantel shelf moulding to the top of the surround. However, to make a neater finish with moulding all round the shelf edge, stick a short length of moulding to each end of the shelf as follows. Mitre the ends of the mantel shelf inwards. Cut two short lengths from mantel-shelf moulding to the same width as the mantel shelf. (When cutting these, check that the moulding is the correct way up so that the moulded edges match.) Mitre the left side on one piece and the right side on the other. Finally, glue the right-hand mitre to the left side of the shelf and the left-hand mitre to the right side of the shelf.

Splatter painting

1 Spray the surround with several coats of primer to obliterate the wood grain.

2 Spray with three coats of pink spray paint.

3 Splatter paint with a coat of grey, then build up the effect by adding a few splatters of black and white.

4 Spray on a coat of splattery pink.

5 Adjust the finished look by adding more speckles of paint as required. It's tempting to keep spraying, but stop when you get a good effect!

6 Finish with a few coats of clear spray lacquer to give a stone-like sheen. (This also has the advantage of preventing the paint chipping, in case future generations should get it into their head to 'play' with your treasures.)

TIP

IT CAN BE TRICKY TO GET THE SIDES LOOKING AS GOOD AS THE FRONT. IF YOU ACCIDENTALLY SPRAY PAINT AN AREA YOU'VE FINISHED, SPRAY IT OVER AGAIN WITH PINK AND RE-SPLATTER.

FURTHER APPLICATIONS

TRADITIONALLY, A FAUX MARBLE EFFECT IS CREATED WITH PAINT WASHES AND VEINING WITH A FEATHER. (FOR MINIATURE WORK, I PREFER TO USE A SPONGE AND FINE PAINT BRUSH.) YOU CAN CREATE AN EQUALLY EFFECTIVE MARBLE EFFECT WITH THE SPLATTER PAINTING TECHNIQUE. IT'S MUCH LESS FIDDLY AND MORE FUN. FOLLOW THE DIRECTIONS FOR GRANITE (LEFT), BUT USE ONLY BLACK (OR GREY) AND WHITE SPRAY PAINT.

Fig 2.9 The splattered paint effect.

TECHNIQUE

Using Filigree Findings

Cheap metal filigrees are useful for making dolls' house accessories. Among other things, they can be used to produce a very convincing plasterwork effect or to imitate carved wooden mouldings, which were a popular Georgian wall decoration. This type of decoration was also used in the Victorian era and became very popular again with the Edwardians. You may think painting over pre-cast filigrees is a cheat. However, in the late 1700s and early 1800s British architects, including the renowned Robert Adam, weren't above painting over small motifs cast in pewter or papier-mâché to resemble rich architectural carving.

Metal filigrees are more commonly used in the hobby of egg crafting. Mail-order egg-crafting suppliers have catalogues with literally hundreds of designs to choose from. (Egg-crafting suppliers can be found in craft magazines.) Choose any that resemble acanthus leaves, scrolls, swags, ribbons, laurels, garlands or clusters of flowers.

PROJECT

Georgian Chimney Breast

This plaster effect is created with white car spray primer. This is matt and has a slightly rough texture when several coats are applied. Generally, period plasterwork would have been painted. The details of the mouldings were sometimes painted in bright pastel colours, or alternatively, painted in a colour toning with the main colour and gilded (highlighted in gold). Standard, ready-made wooden fireplace surrounds are available cheaply from dolls' house shops or mail-order suppliers. Alternatively, make up your own surround following the instructions in the previous project (page 14). If your room doesn't have a built-in chimney breast you can easily add one. Cut a section of scrap wood or thick card the same height as the room and 1–2in (25–51mm) wider than the fire surround. Cut a rectangular opening at the bottom end of this. This will form the front of the chimney breast. Next, cut two strips for the sides to the same height as the front

GEORGIAN CHIMNEY BREAST.

and 1–2in (25–51mm) wide. Glue the sides to the front, then glue this in place on the wall, with the rectangular opening at the base. The best location for the chimney breast is lined up more or less with the chimney outside!

Materials

- ◆ Thick card (e.g. the back of a pad)
- ◆ Selection of small metal filigrees
- ◆ Tacky glue
- ◆ Cheap wooden fire surround
- ◆ Spray primer: white
- ◆ Emulsion paints: pale yellow, golden yellow
- ◆ Gold marker pen
- ◆ Acrylic paint: black and brown

METHOD

Assembling the plasterwork

1 Cut the thick card the same size as the chimney breast.

2 Glue the wooden fireplace centrally at the bottom of the card. (You can customize the fireplace surround with wooden mouldings or decorative strips. I used sections of dowel and a few tiny filigrees.)

3 Arrange the 'plasterwork' filigrees into a decorative pattern on the card, above the fire surround (see Fig 2.10). The pattern should resemble graceful plasterwork. Glue in place with tacky glue.

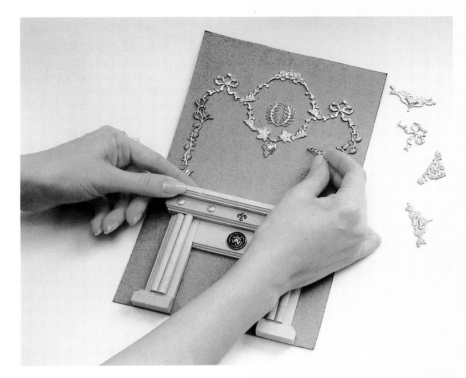

4 Spray the entire assembly with about a dozen thin coats of white spray primer. Allow each coat to dry for 10 minutes between coats. Build up the coats until the grain of the wood is no longer visible and the filigrees blend into the card.

5 Paint the sprayed card (and the rest

Fig 2.10 Placing the filigrees onto the card backing.

Fig 2.11 Priming the assembly.

TIP

GOLD AND SILVER HIGH-
LIGHTER PENS ARE FAR EASIER
FOR THE NON–ARTIST TO USE
THAN A PAINT BRUSH.

FURTHER APPLICATIONS

SEVERAL PLASTERWORK PANELS
CAN BE USED TO MAKE UP A
DECORATIVE FRIEZE (THE AREA
BETWEEN A PICTURE RAIL AND
CORNICE) FOR THE WHOLE
ROOM. A DELICATE GEORGIAN
CEILING CAN ALSO BE MADE
USING THIS METHOD.

*Fig 2.13 Picking out the detail in
dark yellow.*

of the walls in the room) with a
suitable colour such as pale yellow.

Painting the plasterwork

❶ Paint the plaster detail on the card
in a darker tone of the same colour, for
example golden yellow.
❷ Pick out the details on the
plasterwork with gold marker pen for
the gilding.

Fig 2.12 Painting the background yellow.

Distressing the surround

❶ To give the fire surround a stone
effect, use a large paint brush to wash
over it with heavily diluted brown/
black acrylic paint.

2.14 Gilding the detail.

CHAPTER THREE

Miniature Décor

Miniature Décor

Once your dolls' house is built, décor comes before furnishing. It pays to take some time to plan your décor carefully to reflect your chosen style or period. Consider floors, walls, ceilings and windows. These are as much a part of the room as the furnishings. Lay floorboards or create a tiled effect with plastic sheeting (see Chapter 7). Fine plaster ceilings and ceiling roses set off furnishings wonderfully. There's also great scope in period curtaining, which is another area often neglected in the dolls' house. Mary Gilliatt's Period Decorating is excellent for period research and decorative inspiration as is Authentic Decor, The Domestic Interior 1620–1920 by Peter Thornton. (Both are intended for full-size houses.)

TECHNIQUE

Using Textured Paper

Anaglypta is a modern version of lincrusta – wallpaper with a hard, embossed surface, which was developed in the mid-1800s to represent carved wood and plasterwork. Anaglypta has come to mean embossed or textured wallpaper that is designed to be painted. It can be used to simulate miniature plasterwork on ceilings or to create friezes below chair rails. Traditional symmetrical patterns work best. Anaglypta is available in decorating stores where you can also buy the small sample pots of emulsion paint required to finish the project below.

TECHNIQUE

Mitreing

To cut cornices accurately you will need a junior hacksaw and a mitre block. A cheap plastic one will do the job.

1 Place the wider side of the cornice, which goes against the ceiling, against one side of the mitre block.

2 Place the saw blade into the appropriate right- or left-sloping slot.

Use cuts sloping inwards (right-sloping slot) to make frames suitable for square or rectangular ceilings and cuts sloping outwards (left-sloping slot) for corners edging such things as chimney breasts.

3 Saw gently all the way through the moulding, holding it steady with your free hand.

DECORATIVE PLASTER CEILING.

MITREING

- Cornices are not symmetrical. The wider side goes against the wall, the other against the ceiling. It won't matter too much if you fix it upside down so long as you cut all the lengths that way. To avoid confusion, mark all the lengths 'W' (for wall) on the wider side and 'C' (for ceiling) on the other.
- Always double-check the position and the angle before cutting the cornice. This will save many wasted lengths of moulding.
- Don't sand the cut; the sharper the cut the better the join will fit.
- If you need to join a length of moulding, cut the joint at an angle. This is less conspicuous than a straight-cut joint.

PROJECT

Decorative Plaster Ceiling

You'll soon develop a painful crick in your neck if you try to work directly onto your dolls' house ceiling. Nor would I recommend working on the ceilings before you construct the house. A better idea is to make a false ceiling from thin, plain white card. Large sheets are available from stationers. A false ceiling has the added advantage of hiding the electrics, and enabling you to change the décor easily, should you wish.

Cornice mouldings are available from specialist dolls' house suppliers in lengths of 12 and 18in (305 and 457mm). This project also includes the mitreing technique which every DIY miniaturist needs to know.

Materials

- Newspaper
- Thin white card
- Sample of Anaglypta
- Cornice moulding
- Tacky glue
- Narrow lace (optional)
- Emulsion paint
- Gold marker pen (optional)

Fig 3.1 Gluing the Anaglypta to the ceiling card.

METHOD

Fitting the Anaglypta and cornice

1 Make a newspaper template of the ceiling.

2 Cut the card to fit the ceiling exactly.

3 Cut out a suitable section from the

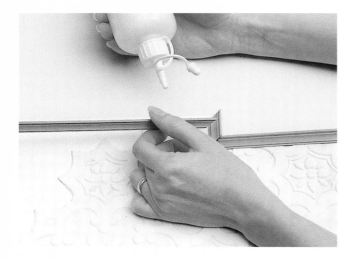

Fig 3.2 Gluing on the cornice.

Fig 3.3 Gluing on embroidered tulle for decoration.

Anaglypta sample. Position the section so that the pattern is central on the card.

4 Spread tacky glue thinly over the back of the Anaglypta and press it onto the card. Make sure it makes good contact while it dries (but don't squash the pattern).

5 Cut, fit and glue the cornice to the three edges of the ceiling. Cornice is generally not fitted to the edge of the dolls' house ceiling with the missing wall.

Period ceiling styles

♦ **Jacobean** Decorate grand rooms with artwork. Plasterwork ceilings were generally painted in bold colours or gilded. Sheets of square plastic tile separators make an effective Jacobean ceiling. Glue a small jump-ring and a small bead to each intersection to simulate the pendants. Glue a decorative filigree to the centre of each square. Apply a couple of coats of off-white emulsion or pick out the details in paint and gild.

♦ **Georgian** Dentil (resembling a row of teeth) or egg and dart mouldings are appropriate on Georgian cornices. Ceilings were generally coated with a whitening made from crushed chalk. Alternatively, use pastel green, blue, pink or dove grey. Gilding is appropriate. (During the French Empire period, 1799–1815, it was fashionable to paint grand bedroom ceilings to resemble a blue sky with wispy clouds.)

♦ **Regency** Ceilings should be plain white without gilding.

♦ **Early Victorian** The typical Victorian ceiling had a central ceiling rose. Paint this a paler shade of the wall colour. Dove grey or washed out green is appropriate for upstairs. Deep cranberry was popular in the dining room. Cornices should be painted a shade darker than the ceiling, but not gilded.

♦ **Late Victorian** Ceilings should not be white, but cream, stone or pastel shades.

♦ **Edwardian** Paint the ceiling creamy white.

Fig 3.4 The ceiling painted a cranberry shade.

KNOW-HOW
CEILINGS

◆ When ordering cornice moulding, remember that it only needs to be fitted to three walls.

◆ Measuring room dimensions is fiddly in a confined space, especially since dolls' house walls, floors and ceilings are not always made up of true right angles. A quick way to find the exact size of an area is to make a newspaper template. Press a sheet of newspaper into the corners and score round carefully with a sharp pencil.

◆ Cornice mouldings come in different widths. As a general guide, use thin cornice on the top floors and below stairs (if you use any at all), medium cornice on the second floor and the largest and most ornate cornice in the hall and main rooms.

◆ To make the grandest rooms really splendid, you can decorate the cornice to resemble fine plasterwork. Glue a length of narrow lace onto the cornice (I used narrow embroidered tulle) and paint with three thin coats of emulsion. Stipple the paint well into the lace so that it is no longer visible.

◆ In a period setting, if the wall is panelled, the cornice should be the same colour as the panelling. Otherwise, it should match the ceiling.

◆ Grand rooms might have gilded plasterwork.

Plasterwork and gilding

1 Glue the narrow lace onto the cornice with plenty of tacky glue. Set aside to dry.

2 Paint the cornice and ceiling with three coats of thinned emulsion paint in an appropriate colour. Mine is the cranberry shade seen in fashionable Victorian dining rooms. Stipple the paint well into the lace on the cornice so that it blends it in.

3 Highlight the details of the plaster ceiling with gold marker pen.

Fig 3.5 Gilding the pattern with a gold pen.

ALTERNATIVE MATERIALS

WHILE PAPER OR FOIL DOILIES LACK THE NECESSARY DEPTH TO MAKE A DEFINED PLASTER CEILING, PLASTIC DOILIES CAN WORK WELL. GLUE ONTO THE CEILING CARD AND SPRAY THEM WITH SEVERAL THIN COATS OF WHITE PRIMER. (EMULSION TENDS TO CLOG UP THE PATTERN.) FABRIC WITH A RAISED EMBROIDERED PATTERN CAN ALSO BE PAINTED TO SIMULATE LINCRUSTA.

KNOW-HOW

WOOD STRIP

- Use a mitre block to cut wood strip and mouldings. This ensures a straight edge.
- You can cut your own veneer strips from veneer sheet.

KNOW-HOW

FLOORBOARDS

- In full-size houses, floorboards lay across joists, so the boards would be side-on when viewed from the front of the house.
- The easiest way to measure the area for making the false cardboard floor is to make a newspaper template. (See Ceilings Know-how, page 23.)
- It is easiest to lay floorboards onto a cardboard base first and then to fit this into the room setting. This false floor is also useful for concealing electrical connections.
- Grey cereal box cardboard is fine for a false floor, but don't use light or brightly coloured card; this tends to show through any gaps in the floorboards.
- Use whatever length of floorboard you like, but bear in mind the overall pattern of the planking. Strips of uninterrupted planking don't look authentic; we expect to see joins in floorboards.
- Don't cut all your floorboards to the same length: plan the joins so that there's a long length followed by a short length, and reverse this on the adjacent row. This way the joins will be well spaced.

continued on page 26

TECHNIQUE

Using Wood Strip

Various sizes of wood strip are available from dolls' house suppliers, model ship making suppliers, hobby shops and mail-order suppliers (see page 146). Wood strip varies in thickness from ¼in (6mm) planks to delicate veneer strip, in dark or light wood. It is useful to keep a selection for making and trimming miniatures. Strips can be cut to size and glued together to make simple slatted kitchen furniture such as tables, stools and cupboards. They can also be used to make slatted beds, wall panelling and wainscots.

PROJECT

Wooden Floorboards

Floorboards are appropriate for most dolls' house rooms, but the kitchen is an exception; it should have a slate or stone floor. Floorboards are easily made with wood strip. Any suitable 10 x 2in (254 x 51mm) wood strip can be used, and cheap packs of second-quality pine strips are available from some mail-order suppliers. One pack will cover several floors, and pine can be stained to resemble any wood.

Generally, it is best to cut wood strip carefully with a junior hacksaw. However, when laying several floors with cheap pine strips the project will progress much faster with power scissors. Miniature skirting will give the

Materials

- Newspaper
- Pine wood strips, pack of 10 x 2in (254 x 51mm)
- Skirting moulding
- Wood glue
- Medium thickness grey or brown cardboard
- Wood stain
- French polish

WOODEN FLOORBOARDS.

finishing touch to your polished wooden floor. It will also neaten the edges and hide the false floor join. Skirting moulding is available from dolls' house suppliers in 12 and 18in (305 and 457mm) lengths. There are different skirting mouldings available for Georgian, Victorian and modern settings.

METHOD

Cardboard base

1 Make a newspaper template of the floor (see Ceilings Know-how, page 23), then use this to cut out a false cardboard floor.

2 Check that the false floor fits, then mark the 'topside' and the 'underside'.

Floorboards

1 Decide on a suitable length for the floorboards. Cut a piece this length from the wood strip and mark it as template 1.

2 Lay this template along the back edge of the cardboard base. Measure the remaining uncovered length of the base and cut a shorter length of wood strip to fit. Mark this as template 2.

3 Cut two dozen or so lengths from each template, making sure they are all uniform.

Laying the floorboards

1 Glue a long length along the back edge of the cardboard 'topside', then glue a short length in place to join the first. This makes the first row.

2 Lay a short length followed by a long length to make the second row.

3 Continue to lay rows of floorboards following the above pattern until the cardboard is completely covered. (Be careful not to get glue on the front of the floorboards.) Set aside to dry.

4 Sand the boards to a fine, smooth finish with fine-grade sandpaper, sanding along the grain.

WOODEN FLOORBOARDS.

Finishing

1 Coat the floorboards with wood stain. (I used Georgian Light Oak.) Set aside to dry.

2 Mark a tiny indent, with a blunt pencil, into the end of each board to imitate nail heads.

3 Coat the floorboarding with two or three coats of french polish, allowing each coat to dry for 10 to 15 minutes before applying the next. Set aside to dry completely.

Fig 3.6 Cutting and laying the floorboards onto card.

continued from page 24

- If you're laying all the floorboards at once, you can plan them to run through doorways and into the next room. If you do this, cut separate cardboard floors for each room and glue the adjoining floorboards onto them only after the final permanent fitting.

- Don't get glue onto the upper surface of the floorboards. Glue will prevent the stain from penetrating the wood. If you are a messy gluer, stain the wood strips before gluing them down.

- Grander rooms would have more expensive wood flooring than the other rooms in a house. Floorboards for these can be stained to resemble ebony (a very precious wood), mahogany, walnut or, more commonly, various shades of oak.

- Upstairs and below stairs rooms, such as bedrooms, nurseries and servants' rooms, were floored using cheaper woods, such as fir or pine, and should be stained accordingly.

- Victorian bedroom and nursery floors were often left unvarnished so that they could be scrubbed with a lime-based disinfectant. (This was because the Victorians discovered 'germs' and consequently developed a mania for hygiene.) To simulate this effect in the dolls' house, scrub over the unvarnished floorboards with dilute grey emulsion paint and a toothbrush. Furniture can also be limed using this technique.

Fig 3.7 Staining the floorboards.

Skirting

1. Position the floor in the room, but do not yet fix in place.
2. Cut, fit and glue the skirting mouldings round the three edges of the floorboards while the floor is in place.
3. Remove the floor, complete with skirting, then stain and polish the skirting to match the flooring.

Fig 3.8 Adding the nail marks.

FURTHER APPLICATIONS

PARQUET FLOORING (REGULAR, GEOMETRIC WOODBLOCK FLOORING) CAN BE MADE WITH THINNER WOOD STRIP IN A SIMILAR WAY. IT ISN'T ANY MORE DIFFICULT, BUT IT TAKES LONGER BECAUSE THE BLOCKS ARE SMALLER. BE SURE TO CUT ALL THE WOODEN BLOCKS THE SAME LENGTH, GLUE THEM TOGETHER TO MAKE PARQUET SQUARES AND THEN FIT THESE TOGETHER TO MAKE UP A REGULAR PATTERN.

Stencilling on Fabric

Small-print fabrics are available for the miniaturist, but still more satisfaction can be had by making your own patterned fabrics with stencils: you can then customize fabrics to a certain period. Before automation, all fabrics were handwoven or handpainted, so this method is also more authentic.

Yellow fleurs-de-lis stencilled onto blue fabric would be appropriate for Georgian fabric. A pink rosebud on green fabric would make an attractive Victorian print. Choose any naturalistic shape for an Art Nouveau or Edwardian effect. For the Regency curtain below, I used an arrowhead design that is typical of the period.

Although stencils can be cut from any thin card, clear acetate sheet is ideal because you can see the fabric through the stencil. Sheets of acetate are available from stationers and dolls' house shops. The design can be spray painted or stippled on with acrylic paint.

Regency Curtains

Dolls' house curtaining is often neglected, but is a wonderful area for the miniaturist to explore. We can do better than a bunched-up square of uninspiring fabric.

The Regency period had the most wonderful window treatments, and curtains were light and gauzy, which is ideal for dolls' house curtains since the thinner the fabric the better they drape.

For this project I used a fine, burgundy cotton handkerchief from a charity shop. Handkerchiefs have the advantage of beautiful, tiny, ready-made hems. The pelmet fabric was from a square sold for patchwork quilting and the trimmings are a snippet of lampshade gimp (trim) and specialist miniature picot braid (available from specialist dolls' house haberdashers: see Suppliers, page 146). The curtain tie-backs are long metal filigrees bent in half. Any similar filigree can be used.

METHOD

Stencilling

1 Make the stencil by drawing or

REGENCY CURTAINS.

Fig 3.9 Cutting out the template with a sharp craft knife.

KNOW-HOW
STENCILLING

- In miniature, simple patterns work best and are easier to cut out.
- Avoid designs that incorporate cut-outs since these are impractical.
- Use a sharp craft knife to cut around the pattern.
- Make the acetate stencil large enough to protect the rest of the fabric when you spray paint.
- If stippling acrylic paint onto the stencil, use a small fat brush with short bristles. Blot the brush nearly dry before applying the paint.
- The finished piece will look more professional if you take time to space the patterns uniformly. You can do this quickly and easily by drawing a grid to show through the fabric. If your fabric is opaque, stick string to the grid-lines and *feel* where the next pattern should be placed.
- Wipe excess paint off the stencil periodically to prevent paint build-up which may smudge onto the fabric.
- The most suitable metallic spray paint is a light, fast-drying craft paint rather than cellulose car spray paint which is too thick to give the lightness required for a stencilled effect.
- The finished project won't be laundered so there's no need to heat seal the design before making up the curtains.

Fig 3.10 Spraying the design onto fabric.

tracing a suitable shape onto a 7in (178mm) square of acetate, with a fine marker pen.

2 Carefully cut around the shape with a sharp craft knife. Press out and discard the central shape.

3 Make a simple measuring grid by marking square inches on the squared paper in thick marker pen so that they show through the fabric. Pin the fabric onto the squared paper.

4 Press the stencil firmly onto the crossing point of the squares seen through the bottom left-hand corner of the fabric. (Reverse for left-handed

Materials

- Thin cotton fabric, e.g. handkerchief (for curtains)
- Striped cotton fabric (for pelmet)
- Sheet of squared paper
- Spray paint: gold
- Spray starch
- Sheet of acetate
- Lampshade gimp (trim) to tone
- Embroidery thread to tone
- Thin brass rod
- ⅛in (3mm) wooden dowel
- Milliput
- Turned brass beads x 3
- Brass jump rings x 10
- Long, metal filigree leaves x 2
- Fine marker pen
- Thick marker pen
- Double-sided tape

workers.) Shake and spray with just a couple of short bursts of gold spray paint. Lift up the stencil. Repeat on the next position. After spraying a few of the designs, wipe the stencil with kitchen paper to prevent a build up of paint.

5 Continue until the whole handkerchief is covered with patterns.

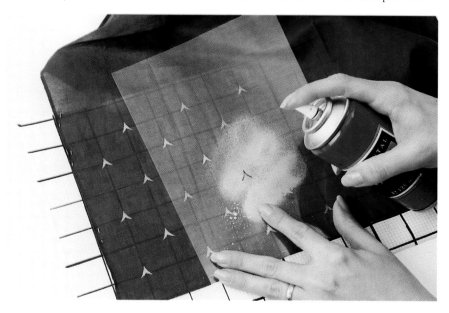

TIP

IF YOUR SPRAY PAINT IS SLOW-
DRYING, BE CAREFUL NOT TO
SMUDGE THE DESIGN AS YOU
WORK.

Curtains

1 Cut two curtain lengths from the fabric so that the top and side seams of the handkerchief make the bottom and side seam of the curtain.

2 Hem the other side of each curtain so that their width is the same as the windows.

3 Cut the thin brass rod to fit the inside width of the window surround, making it just a shade long so that it will wedge into place.

4 Hem the top edge of each curtain 1in (25mm) longer than the required length. Turn the extra inch (25mm) over, sew a small hem to hold it in place, then thread the brass curtain rod in.

5 Saturate the curtains with spray starch on both sides, shape into folds and hang on the clothes line to dry. (Use paper clips in place of pegs.) The finished curtains will be quite stiff to the touch, but they will look very natural when fixed over the window.

6 Wedge the curtains and rod into the window surround.

7 Bend the filigree leaves in half and secure one side to the wall with double-sided tape.

8 Hook the curtains behind the filigree tie-backs and arrange the folds (see photo of finished curtains on page 27).

Pelmet

1 Cut the pelmet fabric 2in (51mm) longer than the width of the window surround so that it gathers gently to cover the curtain. (Heavy trim, such as lampshade gimp, is too bulky to gather much and still drape well.)

2 Fold the fabric in half and cut a

Fig 3.11 Hemming the curtain.

gentle curve in the pelmet fabric so that the curve matches on both sides.

3 Neatly hem both ends.

4 Fold the top edge of the pelmet over to the wrong side, and stitch the brass jump rings along the edge, gathering a little fabric at each ring as you stitch.

5 Stitch the lampshade gimp along the base, following the curve of the pelmet. (I also added some picot braid.)

Curtain pole

1 Cut the wooden dowel 1in (25mm) longer than the width of the window surround.

2 Spray the dowel with a couple of coats of gold spray paint and set aside to dry.

3 Slip half the curtain rings of the pelmet onto the curtain pole, thread on a turned brass bead, then slip on the remainder of the rings.

4 Thread a turned brass bead onto each end of the pole.

5 Mix a small ball of Milliput. Shape

KNOW-HOW

CURTAINS

◆ Natural fabrics, such as cotton and silk, drape much better than synthetics.

◆ Cut curtain fabric twice the width of the window.

◆ Charity shops are a cheap source of fine cotton fabric in the form of handkerchiefs. Keep a look out for the colour ones. (Don't worry, most fancy handkerchiefs have never been used!)

◆ Draping is very important when working with fabric in miniature. Achieve the effects of folds and a feeling of weight with a liberal spray of starch.

◆ To contrive precise folds or pulled-back pleats, as required for a portière curtain (door curtain) or below a draped dressing table, paint the fabric with a fabric stiffening medium such as Stiffy or Get Set. Drape the fabric carefully into place and leave to dry. It will dry rock hard, but will retain its drape.

ABOVE: *Fig 3.12 Sewing the trim and jump rings onto the pelmet.*

ABOVE RIGHT: *Fig 3.13 Modelling the curtain pole ends with Milliput.*

FURTHER APPLICATIONS

STENCILLING NEEDN'T BE CONFINED TO FABRIC. IT CAN BE USED TO EQUALLY GOOD EFFECT ON WALLS OR PAINTED FURNITURE.

an arrowhead onto each end of the pole and set aside to dry.

6 Once the arrowheads have hardened, spray them with gold spray paint. Set aside to dry. The rings won't come off now unless you open them with pliers.

Decorative cording

1 Twist a long length of embroidery thread so that it coils back on itself. To do this, secure one end of the thread and twist the other end until it's tightly wound. Then grip the centre and allow the threads to coil round each other.

2 Tie a knot in the end of the coil to secure it. Fray and trim this into a tassel.

3 Glue one end of this cord to one brass bead, loop and thread the cord through the third curtain hook, then loop and glue to the central brass bead, allowing the end to hang down. Tie this off and fray to make a second tassel. Trim the tassel ends neatly.

4 Repeat steps 2 and 3 on the other side of the pelmet.

5 Saturate the pelmet and cording with spray starch on both sides. Shape into folds and hang to dry.

6 Fix the pelmet over the window by securing the brass beads to the window surround with Milliput.

Fig 3.14 Adding the decorative cording.

CHAPTER FOUR

Decorative
Paint Techniques

Decorative Paint Techniques

Painting furniture may sound like a dubious idea. True enough, slapping a coat of paint on miniature furniture is unlikely to give an attractive effect, but paint is an extremely versatile medium: used judiciously, it can transform an uninspiring piece of furniture into something spectacular.

Acrylic paint can be bought at any art or craft shop. Sets of small tubs, for the craft worker, are an inexpensive way to begin your collection. Test pots of emulsion are available in DIY stores. Choose matt unless you want a shiny finish.

Water-based paints such as acrylics and emulsions give the best results for the amateur because they are very easy to work with. The exception is a metallic finish. While water-based metallics are easier to work with, I find solvent-based paints give a glossier, more metallic finish.

TECHNIQUE

Patination

Patination describes the effect air has on the surface of a metal, especially bronze and copper, turning it a bright blue-green. It is also used to describe the effect used on other metals and wood to give the impression that they are old or antique. Verdigris is another term used to describe the blue-green coating on copper, bronze and brass.

This effect is simulated on modern reproductions. There are full-size DIY kits available from craft suppliers for this purpose, but it's easily achieved with a combination of acrylic and emulsion paint. It is enjoyable to disguise cheap plastic or metal objects by simulating an antique patina.

PROJECT

Victorian Jardinière

This Victorian 'bronze' jardinière is made from two cheap plastic cake decorations. Egg crafting suppliers also stock ranges of similar types of cheap decorations which are great fun to dress up. I used pale green matt emulsion to simulate the patina on bronze. The figure is mounted on two suitably sized buttons. Buttons make excellent mounts and finish off a project very well.

The jardinière is designed to hold a pot plant. I've made various pot plants from green paper, green electrical tape and tiny dried foliage. A type of decorative seaweed sold in florists as air fern makes an attractive miniature display, but keep the foliage off fabrics; the green isn't colourfast and can stain fabric and upholstery.

METHOD

Attaching the pot

1 The bell will become the pot to hold the plant. Glue the bell, upturned, to the cherub's hands so that the figure holds it upright. (You may need to

VICTORIAN JARDINIÈRE.

Materials

- Large plastic cake decoration cherub
- Large plastic cake decoration bell
- Thick button, to fit diameter of cherub base
- Thin button, of roughly the same diameter
- Spray primer
- Paint: bronze
- Matt emulsion paint: pale green
- Blu-tack
- Tea leaves
- Air fern
- Epoxy resin

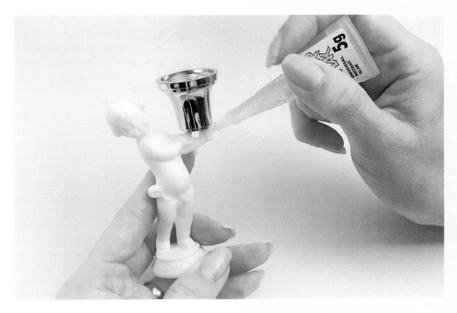

modify your cherub's hands so that he can hold the bell, or even pare off his musical instrument with a craft knife!) Use superglue for an instant bond then reinforce the joint with an epoxy resin such as Araldite. Set the assembly aside to dry.

2 Spray the figure with a coat of primer. Set aside to dry.

3 Paint or spray with two coats of bronze paint. Allow to dry.

The patina

1 Make a patinating wash by diluting the pale green emulsion with a few drops of water.

2 Wash over the figure with the patinating wash. Be sure to fill in all the recesses. Smear the wash over the outer surfaces with your finger. Wipe off the excess paint with a soft cloth and buff to a shine. Once you are pleased with the effect, leave to dry.

Fig 4.2 Priming the assembly.

Fig 4.1 Gluing the bell to the cherub's hands.

KNOW-HOW
PAINTINGS

- Most projects benefit from a coat of spray primer. This levels out the surface and helps the subsequent layers of paint adhere. An economical source of primer is car spray paint.
- Use white primer for pale colours and grey or red for black and dark shades.
- Use acrylic or emulsion paint as the base coat on furniture. Emulsion is more economical, but the acrylic colour range is better.
- Acrylics are the thinnest of the paint types and therefore the best for 'fine painting' such as painting designs onto furnishings.
- Special effects can be achieved with water-based paints applied over specialist media such as Quik-crackle.
- Dilute emulsions and acrylics can be used as a colour wash to add a patina to ornaments and furnishings.

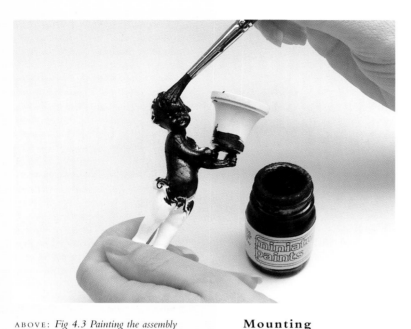

ABOVE: *Fig 4.3 Painting the assembly bronze.*

ABOVE RIGHT: *Fig 4.4 Patinating with green emulsion.*

KNOW-HOW
PATINATION

◆ When applying a patina wash, apply it in a similar way to how patina naturally builds up on objects. Polishing removes the patina from the smooth convex surfaces leaving it to build up in the recesses. Copy this effect by rubbing off the patina with a soft cloth before it dries.

◆ If you don't like the effect of your patinating wash, simply rinse it off in hot water before it dries and have another go!

Mounting

1 Glue the figure to the buttons with epoxy resin, ensuring that the buttons are centred before the glue dries.
2 Fill the pot holder with Blu-tack.
3 Press tea leaves on top of the Blu-tack.
4 Make a hole in the centre with a matchstick and push in the base of the fern.
5 Press the Blu-tack and the leaves round the base to secure the plant.
6 Arrange the foliage.

PAINT THE FIGURE 'BRASS' AND PATINATE WITH A DILUTE ACRYLIC PAINT IN A DIRTY BLACK-BROWN SHADE. PROPRIETARY PATINATING FLUIDS (SUCH AS HOME DÉCOR ANTIQUING GEL) CAN ALSO CREATE AN ANTIQUED EFFECT. TRY THE EFFECT ON PICTURE AND MIRROR FRAMES, SMALL ORNAMENTS AND LAMP FITTINGS, AND ON URNS, STATUES, RAILINGS AND COACH LAMPS.

Fig 4.5 Mounting on buttons.

TECHNIQUE
Using Crackle Glaze

Distressing is another technique for making new furniture appear old. There are several ways to get a distressed effect. My favourite technique is to use crackle glaze. This is used in the hobby of egg crafting and is sold in craft shops under several different brand names, including Quik-crackle and Crackle & Age. It's my favourite technique for ageing because it's so enjoyable to do.

The crackle effect can be used on any painted area – walls, furniture, doors, windows and woodwork. A cheap item can appear impressive when intentionally made to look old and well worn. The distressed effect is most effective for rustic, below-stairs or nursery furniture.

PROJECT
Distressed Linen Cupboard

This large cupboard, which came from a cheap set of furniture, seemed an ideal candidate for distressing with crackle glaze. To give the cupboard a more rustic look, I replaced the brass handles with wooden beads pushed onto thin dowel. Instead of replacing the glazing, I finished the cupboard doors with 'wire grille' made from tulle.

METHOD

Preparation
1 Remove the plastic 'glass' and handles from the cupboard.

Materials
- Cheap wooden cupboard
- Small wooden beads
- Thin dowel
- Fine sandpaper
- Emulsion: off-white (or pale) and pink (or mid-tone)
- Crackle glaze
- Patinating medium (or dilute acrylic wash)
- Tulle
- Spray paint: silver
- Tacky glue

2 Sand the cupboard to remove the shiny varnish and key (roughen) the surface so that the paint can adhere.
3 Make wooden handles by pressing the small wooden beads onto thin dowel. Replace the metal handles with these wooden ones.

KNOW-HOW
CRACKLE GLAZE

- Crackle glaze will work with any water-based paint such as emulsion or acrylic paint.
- Practise the technique on scrap wood first since timing the topcoat is important. The glaze must still be tacky when the topcoat is applied.
- Any colour can be painted over any other colour. Matt blue, green or terracotta painted over pale undercoats look particularly effective.
- Apply plenty of glaze. You can paint over too much distressing, but you can't add more later.
- If the glaze doesn't crackle, it was dry before you applied the topcoat.
- If you use shades that are too similar, the crackle effect won't show.

DISTRESSED LINEN CUPBOARD.

CRACKLE GLAZE CAN BE USED ON ITS OWN TO CREATE AN AGED EFFECT ON PAINTINGS. THIS LOOKS ESPECIALLY EFFECTIVE FOR LARGE PAINTED PANELS MOUNTED DIRECTLY ONTO THE WALL TO FORM A FRIEZE. (LOOK OUT FOR SUITABLE PASTORAL SCENE GREETINGS CARDS.) PAINT A THICK BUT EVEN COAT OF CRACKLE GLAZE ONTO THE PICTURE AND AS SOON AS THIS IS TACK DRY, PAINT ON A FURTHER COAT. THE EFFECT CAN BE SEEN AS SOON AS THE SECOND COAT BEGINS TO DRY. RUB OVER WITH PATINATING MEDIUM TO AGE.

4 Apply an undercoat of off-white emulsion. Set aside to dry.

5 Using a fine paint brush, paint the crackle glaze thickly onto sites that would naturally wear; on corners and along the sides and edges of the cupboard.

Painting

1 Using a clean brush, paint over the cupboard with the topcoat (pink emulsion). As you paint, the topcoat will shrink and crack to

Fig 4.6 Sanding the cupboard.

TIP

IF THE CRACKLE EFFECT DOESN'T APPEAR, THE GLAZE HAS BECOME TOO DRY. SAND OFF THE TOPCOAT AND START AGAIN. IT SHOULDN'T AFFECT THE FINISHED RESULT AS LONG AS YOU DON'T HAVE TOO MANY ATTEMPTS ON THE SAME PIECE OF FURNITURE.

Fig 4.8 Painting on the crackle glaze.

Fig 4.7 Painting on the base colour.

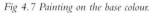

Fig 4.9 Painting on the top colour.

Fig 4.10 Fitting tulle 'wire grilles'.

show the undercoat. The topcoat needs to be applied to the crackle glaze while the glaze is still tacky.

2 Apply a little patinating medium to a soft cloth and gently rub over the cracks to simulate a build-up of grime.

Wire grille

1 Cut sections of tulle to fit the cupboard doors.

2 Spray both sides of the tulle sections with silver spray paint. Set aside to dry.

3 Glue a tulle section over the back of each door with tacky glue. Stretch the tulle tautly across the window so that it resembles wire mesh.

TECHNIQUE
Rosmålning

Rosmålning, or rose painting, is a Scandinavian tradition which dates back to the beginning of the eighteenth century. It was used to decorate traditional, rustic furniture. There is no need to buy expensive brushes to execute it: just raid a relative's make-up bag!

Rosmålning is suitable for chests, trunks, cabinets, tables and chairs. The secret to painting a motif is to do it with confidence. Having said that, don't be afraid to have a go. I'm certainly no artist. The handpainted element of this furniture adds to its rustic charm, so don't worry about trying to get all the motifs on the drawers to match. Just have fun painting and I guarantee the effect will be pleasing.

The motif is painted with a wide flat brush (which translates into something like an eyeshadow brush for our purposes) and is outlined with a thin pointed brush (something like an eyeliner brush). As for colours, you can use your own choice of colours to complement the background colour. Deep red-browns, dull greens and strong blues are traditional. This type of furniture was often personalized with initials or dates.

KNOW-HOW
ROSMÅLNING

◆ To make confident brush sweeps, practise the strokes before working on furniture.

◆ Use as few strokes as possible to achieve the pattern.

◆ Don't overdo the painting – less is more.

◆ If you need to tidy up the finished effect, you can refine the line of your motif by over-painting with a little base colour, using a very fine brush.

◆ Furniture decorated with rosmålning can be given a thin coat of matt varnish to protect the finish.

RUSTIC CHEST OF DRAWERS.

PROJECT

Rustic Chest of Drawers

Rosmålning is ideal for cheering up cheap pieces of furniture since they are often already rustic-looking, and a painted finish covers a multitude of sins.

METHOD

Preparation

1 Remove the handles from the chest. (Pull knobs off with pliers or lever handle plates off with an old craft knife.) Sand the chest lightly to remove the shiny varnish and key the surface so that the paint adheres well.

2 Spray the chest and the drawers with a coat of spray primer.

3 Paint with two thin coats of base colour and set aside until completely dry.

Painting the motif

1 Use the wide flat brush to paint on the main motif. The secret here is to use short, confident sweeps rather than lots of fiddly brushing. Begin by painting the yellow background scrolls. Paint the right-hand one (or left-hand

Materials

◆ Chest of drawers
◆ Fine sandpaper
◆ Emulsion or acrylic: base colour
◆ Wide flat brush
◆ Thin pointed brush
◆ Acrylic paints: yellow, red, green and white
◆ Fine black marker pen

one if you are left-handed) as it comes naturally to you, beginning at the dot and sweeping round the centre of the drawer to finish. The second stroke is a little more tricky, as the opposing scroll must be painted on the other side. If you aren't satisfied with the effect, quickly wipe off the paint with a damp cloth before it dries and have another go. They don't have to match exactly!

2 Paint a red dog rose in the centre of each drawer. Paint five petals, each made up of two strokes of the brush.

3 Paint a green leaf, made up of two

Fig 4.11 Removing the original drawer handles.

Fig 4.12 Priming the cupboard.

Fig 4.13 Painting on the blue base coat.

strokes of the brush, on either side of
the rose. On the larger drawers, paint
an additional stem with three tiny
leaves.

Outlining in white

1 Highlight one side of each rose petal
with white paint using the fine brush.
2 Add some highlights to the leaves.
(You can also add 'whiskers' in the
spaces, paint stamens on the flowers and
add dots or 'pearls' round the edge.)

Fig 4.15 Adding the white highlights.

Outlining in black

1 Using the fine black marker pen,
outline some of the motif in black.
Cross-hatching (a criss-cross pattern)
can be added to larger areas such as
flowers and teardrops. Dots can be
added around the motif.

VARIAIONS

PAINTING TECHNIQUES CAN BE
COMBINED TO GOOD EFFECT.
A CHEST OF DRAWERS
DISTRESSED WITH CRACKLE
GLAZE CAN THEN BE DECORATED
WITH ROSMÅLNING.

Fig 4.14 Painting on the basic design.

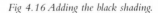

Fig 4.16 Adding the black shading.

TROMPE L'ŒIL

- To get the best results, study the highlights and shadows in pictures or photos of the look you want to simulate.
- Pay attention to perspective in 'outside' scenes.
- Use naturalistic colours. Garish shades will give the game away.

TECHNIQUE

Trompe l'Œil

Trompe l'œil (pronounced tromp loy) simply means 'fool the eye'. It is a painting technique which gives the illusion of something solid, and can be used to fake wood panels, curtains or even books in a bookcase. It's not a dolls' house cheat at all, but a well-respected art form dating back to fifteenth-century Italy. It's fun to try and the finished effects can be very impressive.

Trompe l'œil does require some artistic ability, but with a bit of practice, it's soon picked up. To get a realistic effect you need to be aware of the effects of light and shade on the objects you are representing. It's a bit like painting in 3-D. Start with something simple and straightforward such as the quilted effect in the Quilted Screen project. This effect could also be used for the back of a four-poster bed where the shadows will enhance the effect.

The Quilted Screen project also demonstrates a simple method of hinging for the unskilled woodworker (like me). Hinging is considerably less fiddly if you glue the hinge in place with superglue before fixing the nails. As for the nails, I prefer to use cut-down dressmakers' pins – they are as fine as miniature nails and much cheaper.

PROJECT

Quilted Screen

You're sure to find a corner in your dolls' house for this timeless screen. It will sit happily in any room and any period setting, from Georgian to present day. The quilting effect is achieved by mixing four shades of a

Materials

- ⅛in (3mm) wood sheet
- Fine sandpaper
- Spray primer: grey
- Acrylic or matt emulsion paints: blue, black, white and gold
- Squared paper
- Thick pencil
- Masking tape
- Small piece of sponge
- Tiny brass hinges x 4
- Superglue
- Dressmakers' pins x 4

single colour paint. This makes sense because the effect simulates a single sheet of quilted fabric. I used very light blue for the fabric colour, light blue for the fabric shading, mid-blue for shadowed areas and white-blue for highlighted areas.

METHOD

The screen

1 Cut three matching panels from the

QUILTED SCREEN.

wood sheet, 5 x 1½in (127 x 38mm). Using fine sandpaper, lightly sand the panels to a smooth finish, ready for painting.

② Coat each panel on both sides with a few coats of grey primer to obliterate the wood grain.

③ Mix all the paint shades required: light blue, white-blue, mid-blue and dark blue.

④ Paint the panels on both sides with an even coat of very light blue paint and set aside to dry.

Quilting effect

① On squared paper mark out a grid of ⅝in (16mm) squares in thick pencil.

② Turn the grid so that the squares become diamonds and place it, pencil-side down, onto one of the painted wooden panels. Line up the top of the panel with the top of the central diamond and secure temporarily with masking tape.

③ Rub over the grid gently with the pencil to transfer the pattern to the panel. Repeat on the remaining two panels so that they all match.

④ Lightly stick a strip of masking tape onto the top, right-sloping grid-line on one of the panels.

⑤ Sponge along the straight edge of the tape in light blue paint.

⑥ When dry (this will take only a minute or two), carefully peel the tape off and move it down to the grid line below. Repeat the process and continue until all the right-sloping lines have been sponged.

⑦ Repeat steps 4–6 on the left-sloping grid lines.

Highlighting and shadowing

① Paint or sponge (whichever you find easier) white-blue into the top corner of each diamond. This gives a padded effect as if light is falling from above.

② Sponge mid-blue onto the base of each diamond to give a 3-D, padded effect.

Fig 4.19 Sponging on the shading over masking tape.

ABOVE LEFT: *Fig 4.17 Priming and painting the screen panels.*

ABOVE: *Fig 4.18 Transferring the grid pattern onto the panels.*

KNOW-HOW
PAINTING

◆ Mix all the paint shades before you begin painting.

◆ Mix up plenty of paint. It's very difficult to match up a shade if you run out.

◆ The closer the shades, the subtler the finished effect.

◆ When applying paint with a sponge, blot the sponge beforehand.

Fig 4.20 Panels showing shading (centre);
highlighting (left); shading and highlighting
(right).

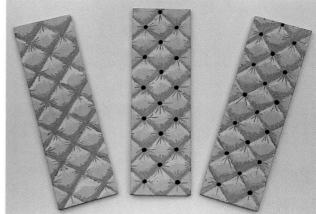

Fig 4.21 Panels showing painted fabric folds
(left); buttons (centre); and gold upholstery
pins (right).

FURTHER APPLICATIONS

IN THE MINIATURE WORLD,
TROMPE L'OEIL CAN BE USED
TO SIMULATE VIEWS OF EXTERIOR
OR INTERIOR SCENES.
A POPULAR USE OF TROMPE
L'OEIL IN BOTH FULL-SIZE AND
MINIATURE DECORATION IS THE
SHELF-FULL-OF-BOOKS EFFECT
CONCEALING A DOOR TO A
SECRET PASSAGE OR A WALL SAFE
... NOW THERE'S A THOUGHT!

THE TROMPE L'OEIL TECH-
NIQUE GIVEN ABOVE CAN BE
ADAPTED TO GIVE A FINISH
SIMULATING BRICK OR YORK
STONE ON THE EXTERIOR OF A
DOLLS' HOUSE. PAINT THE WALL A
MORTAR COLOUR. STICK ON
THIN LINES OF MASKING TAPE TO
PROTECT THE MORTAR LINES,
THEN SPONGE ON THE BRICK OR
STONE EFFECT USING VARIOUS
COLOURS OF MATT EMULSION.

Folds

1 Using light blue paint and a fine paint brush, paint a couple of short dashes radiating from the intersections of each diamond to represent creased folds.

2 Using an improvised tool, such as the flat end of an orange stick, dipped into dark blue paint, print a button at each diamond intersection.

3 In the same fashion, print upholstering pin markings in gold around the edge of the panel, this time using the head of a dressmakers' pin.

TIP

AS YOU ARE HINGING THE SCREEN, BE SURE TO FIX ALL THE PANELS TOGETHER WITH THE HIGHLIGHTED DIAMONDS UPWARDS, OR THE QUILTED EFFECT WILL BE LOST.

Hinging the screen

1 Measure and mark 1in (25mm) up from the top and 1in (25mm) down from the base of one panel. Superglue a hinge below the top mark and above the lower mark.

2 Firmly press a sharp pin into the nail holes of each hinge, holding the pin with blunt-nosed pliers.

3 Snip the point off the pin so that it measures about ⅛in (3mm) in length and push it into the nail hole of the hinge with the end of the pliers.

TIP

BE SURE TO PRESS THE PIN IN STRAIGHT DOWN, SO THAT IT DOESN'T PROTRUDE THROUGH THE ARTWORK.

4 Repeat with the remaining nail holes for the hinges on the first panel.

5 Line up the second panel with the first panel's hinges and fix the hinge in position using the same technique.

6 Fix the last panel in the same way, but remember that it must hinge the opposite way from the first panel so that the finished screen makes a z-shape.

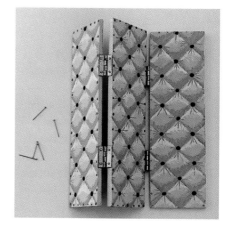

Fig 4.22 Hinging the screen.

CHAPTER FIVE

Metal
Miniatures

CHAPTER FIVE

Metal Miniatures

Where possible I like to use the appropriate medium for making a miniature: sometimes metal is required. The first stop for mini metal components is the K&S Metal Center stand, often seen in hobby shops. Metal Center products are also available mail order from Hobby's Annual. The stand includes metal tubing, thin sheet, channels, rods, wires and angles. It's also worth collecting odd metal bits and bobs as well as jewellery findings and metal filigrees.

TECHNIQUE
Painting Metal Furniture

Cheap, imported white metal furniture, like cheap wooden furniture, is often seen in dolls' house shops, fairs and gift shops. The most common type is made from closely coiled metal. It is approximately 1/12 scale, finely detailed and available in a wide range of designs. Simpler imported metal accessories,

such as bird cages, bicycles and prams, can also be found in gift shops and in flea markets, often with a white, blue, pink or black finish. White metal furniture can be attractive, but identical to other collectors' pieces. It's fun and easy to customize this furniture and give it a completely new look.

KNOW-HOW
PAINTING METAL

- Always undercoat metal furniture with primer. The top coat will then go on more smoothly and adhere better.
- Much metal furniture can be transformed by adding cushions or upholstery.

PROJECT
Peacock Chair

White metal furniture lends itself to being painted to imitate bamboo furniture, garden furniture and black and gold bedsteads, but I wanted to try something different. This peacock chair wouldn't fit in just anywhere, but it would sit well in an Oriental setting or in a conservatory.

I used a snippet of wide, embroidered cotton braid to make the cushion. Cotton braid isn't as common as it used to be. Nowadays most braid is nylon, but if you keep looking you can still find cotton braid on market stalls

PEACOCK CHAIR.

and in old-fashioned sewing or craft shops. Buy a metre when you see it, to add to your sewing materials. This type of braid has many miniature uses since it resembles miniature cross stitch or embroidery.

The peacock fan is made from a few small peacock feathers I collected from a wildlife park (and yes, a peacock). I simply bound them together with glue and yellow cord and decorated the end with a bead and tassel.

Materials

- ◆ White metal chair
- ◆ Spray primer: grey
- ◆ Acrylic paint: blue, green and yellow
- ◆ Solvent-based paint: gold
- ◆ Clear spray lacquer
- ◆ Dressmakers' pins
- ◆ Wide embroidered cotton braid
- ◆ Sewing thread
- ◆ Stuffing for cushion (kapok or cotton wool)
- ◆ Snippet of double-sided sticky tape

METHOD

Chair

1. Wash, rinse and dry the chair to remove any dust.
2. Coat the chair evenly with several coats of grey spray primer until the coil in the metal is no longer visible.
3. Mix the green and blue paint to make turquoise. Apply two coats to the chair, allowing each coat to dry.
4. Pick out some of the chair's details in gold, yellow, blue and green paint.
5. Spray with clear lacquer to protect the finish.

Cushion

1. Choose a section of pattern on the braid for the cushion front. Mark the centre of the pattern with a pin on the right side.
2. Measure the seat area of the chair. Cut two and a half times this length in braid, keeping the marker pin central.
3. With the braid wrong-side up, fold over ¼in (6mm) at both ends and pin these folds down.
4. Bring both pinned ends to meet over the pin marking the centre. Now check that the cushion will fit the chair

VARIATIONS

METAL FURNITURE OFTEN RESEMBLES WICKER. A WICKER LOOK CAN BE ACHIEVED BY PAINTING THE FURNITURE TO RESEMBLE WICKER OR BAMBOO OR SYSTEMATICALLY WRAPPING THE FURNITURE WITH RAFFIA AND COATING WITH FRENCH POLISH. (SEE CHAIR IN CROSS STITCH ROSE CUSHION, CHAPTER 11, PAGE 130.)

seat. If not, enlarge or decrease its size accordingly.

5 Slip stitch along both sides of the cushion, catching all the braid edges in the stitches. Remove the pins.

6 Turn the cushion right-side out to reveal a perfect instant cushion with a central back opening – we hope! Remove the central pin and gently poke out the corners with a cocktail stick.

7 Stuff the cushion lightly with kapok or cotton wool.

8 Sew up the cushion opening and plump the cushion up.

9 Cut a rectangle of double-sided sticky tape, smaller than the cushion, to fit the chair seat. Stick one side to the chair seat, peel the other side off and stick the cushion to it, with the seam downwards.

Fig 5.5 Making up the cushion.

TECHNIQUE
Using Sheet Metal

Since kitchen ranges are metal, I decided my miniature interpretation should be made of the same medium. Pre-packed sheets of 4 x 10in (102 x 254mm) sheet metal can be found in K&S Metal Centers (see Suppliers, page 146). The brass, copper, aluminium and tin sheets come in a variety of thicknesses.

PROJECT
Kitchen Range

Although there are lots of components in this project, it isn't complicated, and the kitchen range is the focal point of the kitchen so I hope you'll agree the result is well worth following all the steps. You'll then be the proud owner of a miniature kitchen range with opening doors and glowing coals.

Metal is an appropriate medium for a kitchen range, but it has to be thin enough to work. To give the range a bit more 'body' I sprayed it with a whole tin of grey metal primer, building up the finish in several thin coats. Metal sheet suppliers also stock metal tube and rod along with belaying pins. These are used in model shipbuilding, but I find them useful for making tiny turned wooden handles.

The other components are stocked by bead suppliers and hardware stores. Metal sticky tape is sold in dolls' house shops for lighting circuits or in DIY stores for lead-lighting. Superglue for metal is quick and effective but you can also use an epoxy resin.

If your dolls' house is electrified you can fit acrylic light-gathering rods (see Suppliers, page 146) in the 'coals' behind the grill. Illuminate the rods with a 12 volt light bulb. As for miniature coals – I empty the crumbs out of my toaster at regular intervals. If you keep an immaculate toaster and have no charred breadcrumbs, you can achieve a similar effect with spent match heads.

METHOD

Cutting the sheet

1 Trim one 10 x 4in (254 x 102mm) metal sheet to measure 7 x 4in (178 x 102mm).

2 With the sheet lengthways, score a horizontal line across it, 1⅜in (35mm) from the top. Score two vertical lines 1⁵⁄₁₆in (33mm) from each side with a steel rule and craft knife. These are the top and side folds.

3 Lightly score one vertical line 2⅜in (60mm) from the right side and another 3⁵⁄₁₆in (84mm) from the left side and

KNOW-HOW
SHEET METAL

- Thin sheet metal can be cut with power scissors or scored with a craft knife.
- Handle cut metal sheet very carefully – the edges can be lethal to fingers.
- When bending sheet metal, bend away from the scored line over a metal rule. This gives the cleanest finish to the edge.

Materials

Body
- Thin sheet metal, 10 x 4in (254 x 102mm) x 2
- Large metal washers x 2
- ⅝in (16mm) diameter brass tube, 5½in (140mm) long
- Coarse sandpaper
- Superglue
- Large metal rings x 3
- Metal sticky tape (lead or copper)
- ⅛in (3mm) wood strip
- ⅟₁₂in (2mm) brass rod
- Blu-tack
- Decorative filigree, to fit above grate
- Earring clutch
- Butterfly earring fastener
- Pierced spacer
- Small decorative bead 'knobs' x 3
- Tiny brass nails x 5
- Spray primer: grey
- Spray paint: black

Door and hinges
- Thin brass sheet
- Earring clutch
- Blu-tack
- Superglue
- Seed beads x 2
- ⅟₂₅in (1mm) brass rod
- ⅟₁₂in (2mm) brass rod
- Tiny brass nails x 4

Boiler tap
(all components should be brass-coloured except belaying pin)
- ⅟₁₂in (2mm) brass rod
- Tiny jump ring
- Tiny washer
- Tiny seed beads x 2
- Belaying pin
- Tiny eyelet
- Medium jump ring
- Medium washer

Coals
- Acrylic light-gathering rod
- Balsa cement
- Charred breadcrumbs or spent match heads
- 12 volt light bulb

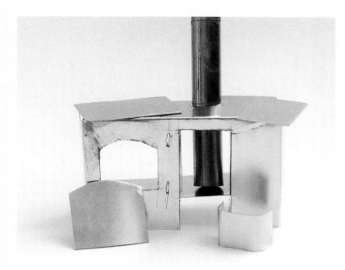

ABOVE: *Fig 5.6 Bending and assembling the basic range structure.*

ABOVE RIGHT: *Fig 5.7 Gluing on the trim, grill and flue.*

BELOW: *Fig 5.8 Priming the range.*

BELOW RIGHT: *Fig 5.9 Spraying the range black.*

deeply score a horizontal line between these lines, ¼in (6mm) down from the horizontal fold.

4 Cut roughly up the middle of the vertical lines drawn in step 3 with power scissors. Wiggle the pieces back and forth until they come cleanly away from the deeply scored line along their top to form flaps.

5 Cleanly bend these flaps back to 90° to form the grate opening.

6 In the horizontal fold above the

grate opening, cut out a circle with old manicure scissors, to fit the metal tube 'flue'. The hole should be positioned in the centre, at the back of the fold (see photo of finished piece).

Oven opening

1 Score on the lines of the oven opening on the left side, 1in (25mm) up from the base, ½in (13mm) down from the horizontal fold, ⅜in (10mm) from the left-hand vertical fold and ½in

(13mm) from the grate opening fold. Drill a hole in the middle and cut out a larger working hole with manicure scissors. Cut along the lower horizontal line as far as the two vertical lines with power scissors. Cut round the rest of the opening, rounding the top edges.

2 Cut two ¼in (6mm) hinge holes to the right of the oven opening, one ⅜in (10mm) and the other 1½in (38mm) down from the top. (Score several times with the point of a sharp craft knife.)

3 Cut out the oven door from the second metal sheet to measure 1½in (38mm) square. Trim one side to a gentle curve.

Bending the shape

1 Cleanly bend both the vertical folds to 90° and snip along the horizontal lines on both of the sides.

2 Bend the range's horizontal fold cleanly to 90° to create two overlapping side flaps.

3 Roughen these flaps with coarse sandpaper and glue them inside the sides with superglue. This will form a half-box structure.

Shelf

1 Make two snips in the grate flaps, ¾in (19mm) up from the base, into which to fit a shelf. Cut the shelf to fit across the inside of the range so that it sits just below the base of the oven door opening (see Fig 5.6). Glue in place.

2 Fit the brass tube 'flue' into the hole on the horizontal fold, with its base resting on the shelf.

Hot plates

1 From the second metal sheet cut two rectangles, 1⅞ x 2⅛in (48 x 54mm) and 1⅞ x 1⅛in (48 x 28mm), to fit on either side of the top of the range.

Ash pan guard

1 Cut out a section of metal sheet,

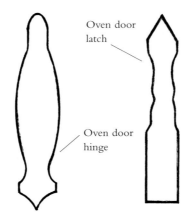

Oven door latch

Oven door hinge

Fig 5.10 Pattern for the hinge pieces.

⅞ x 2in (22 x 51mm).

2 Carefully bend the sides round a thin tube, such as a pen, to shape them to fit the lower grate opening.

Adding decorations

1 Neatly edge the oven door, oven door opening and the top and bottom of the ash pan guard with metal tape.

2 Finish the bottom edge along the right-hand side of the range with metal tape.

3 Cut a length of metal tape down the centre. Stick on an arch-shaped window on the right-hand side of the range, to represent the position of the boiler. Press this down securely.

4 Flatten out one side of the butterfly earring fastener with pliers. Glue it, flattened side pointing up, to the left of the oven opening, halfway down, where the latch will rest.

5 Glue the three large rings, evenly spaced, to the front of the range, along its base.

6 Roughen the backs of the two metal hot plates and glue in place.

7 Glue a washer centrally on top of each hot plate.

Grill

1 Cut two lengths of wood strip to fit horizontally into the grate opening. Temporarily fix the two strips together

TIP

TO EDGE METAL SHEET WITH METAL TAPE, POSITION THE CENTRE OF THE TAPE OVER THE EDGE OF THE SHEET AND PRESS THE TAPE DOWN ON EITHER SIDE. NEATLY EASE THE TAPE ROUND THE CORNERS.

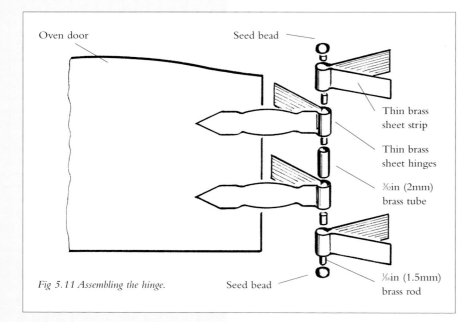

Fig 5.11 Assembling the hinge.

with Blu-tack and drill eight, evenly-spaced holes through both strips.

2 Cut eight 1½in (38mm) lengths from ⅛in (2mm) brass rod.

3 Glue the rods into the drilled wood strips to make a grill with a wood strip at each end.

4 Glue the grill into the top of the grate opening.

5 Glue the decorative filigree above the grill.

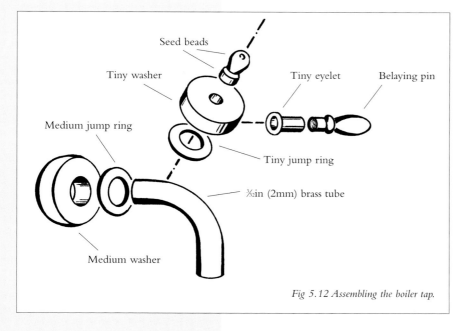

Fig 5.12 Assembling the boiler tap.

Painting

1 Roughen all the surfaces of the range with coarse sandpaper to help paint to adhere.

2 Spray the range, oven door and ash pan guard with a dozen thin coats of grey primer to get a smooth finish. Set aside to dry.

3 Spray with several thin coats of black spray paint.

Brass trim

1 Glue an earring clutch to the centre of the ash pan guard.

2 Glue a tiny decorative bead 'knob' centrally inside each large ring along the front of the range. (See Fig 5.13.)

3 Cut down and glue tiny brass nails into the thread holes of the beads.

4 To make the decorative plate on the oven door, glue the pierced spacer centrally on the door, above the top hinge. Trim down two tiny brass nails and glue the heads into the holes at each end.

Oven door and latch

1 Using the template provided (see Fig 5.10), cut out the oven door latch from the thin brass sheet.

2 Glue an earring clutch to the centre of the latch.

3 Blu-tack the latch in place on the door so that it rests on the butterfly fastening.

4 Cut a strip of brass, ⅛in (3mm) wide. Bend the strip to accommodate the latch, and round off the ends neatly with manicure scissors. Glue over the latch, on the door. (See Fig 5.13.)

Hinge

1 Using the template provided (see Fig 5.10), cut out two hinge strips then cut two plain strips from the thin brass sheet, ¼in (6mm) wide.

2 Cut a 1½in (38mm) length of ¹⁄₂₄in (1mm) thin brass rod. Bend the hinges and the strips centrally over the rod.

3 Cut a ⁵⁄₁₆in (8mm) length of ⅛in (2mm) brass tube.

4 Assemble the hinge on the rod as follows; plain strip, hinge strip, short tube, hinge strip, plain strip. Glue a tiny seed bead onto each end of the ⅟₁₆in (1mm) rod to keep them all in place. (See Fig 5.11.)

5 Glue one side of each hinge strip to the front of the oven door, and the other side of each hinge to the back of the oven door, so that the hinge is positioned correctly. (See Fig 5.13.)

6 Thread the plain strips into the hinge holes to the right of the oven door opening. (Work them bigger with a craft knife until the hinges thread through.) Open out the plain strips on the inside to secure them in place.

Boiler tap

1 Drill a small hole in the centre of the arch shape of the boiler.

2 Bend a section of ³⁄₃₂in (2mm) brass rod to a right angle. Cut away the waste and discard.

3 Glue the tiny jump ring to the top of the bend. Glue the tiny washer to the top of the jump ring.

4 Glue two tiny gold seed beads to the top of the washer.

5 Trim off the end of a belaying pin. Fit it into the tiny eyelet. Glue the flat end of the eyelet to the top washer.

6 Glue the medium jump ring to the back of the rod, followed by the medium washer. Glue this into the hole in the boiler. (See Fig 5.12.)

Coals

1 Cut the acrylic light-gathering rod into 1 or 2in (25 or 51mm) segments. Glue against the grill with balsa cement, concentrating most rods at the base where the coals glow red.

2 Fill in the remaining space with 'coals' (charred breadcrumbs or spent match heads).

3 Glue a 12 volt light bulb to the back of the grill so that it shines into most of the rod ends. (The bulb doesn't have to be glued too neatly since it won't be on view.)

4 Attach the bulb wires to the dolls' house electrical circuit. Switch on, stand back and admire!

LEFT: *Fig 5.14 Fitting the acrylic light-gathering rods.*

TECHNIQUE
Soft Soldering

Soldering is the process of joining metal to metal. Metal components can be joined with epoxy glue such as Araldite or a two-part epoxy putty such as Milliput – the joint can even be painted silver – but you can't beat a soldered joint for strength. And of course, it looks more authentic. Soft soldering is the easiest form of soldering, and brass and copper are the easiest metals to solder. Once you get the hang of soldering, you will probably prefer to solder metals where once you glued. Like all skills, there's an art to soldering and a satisfaction in honing the skill.

As a child, my 3 volt electric dolls' house lamps would sometimes need resoldering. My father would do this with a javelin-sized soldering iron and an industrial blowtorch. I was delighted when my brother-in-law recently lent me a plug-in soldering iron the size of a pencil. For miniature work the smaller the soldering tip, the better.

You'll also need flux. This is a paste and comes in a pot and prevents the metal oxidizing: oxidation prevents a strong bond. Soft solder is also required. This is a metal alloy which melts at a low temperature and it is this that makes the join. I found my supply in my dad's garage. (But there isn't enough for everyone.) It looks like thick silver wire on a big cotton spool (see Fig 5.15). Again, the thinner the better because less solder is deposited onto the iron.

Soldering Technique

1. Thoroughly clean the components to be soldered with fine sandpaper or wire wool and apply some flux to both of the surfaces to be joined.
2. Dip the tip of the iron into the flux.
3. When the iron is hot enough, the flux will melt and sizzle. Touch the tip of the iron onto the solder so that it becomes coated with a blob of molten solder. (This is known as tinning.)
4. Hold the pieces to be joined together and touch the join with the tip of the tinned iron. When the pieces reach the same temperature as the iron, the solder will run into the join. You can usually feel the pieces join.
5. Remove the iron and allow the assembly to cool.
6. Once cool, clean the tip of the soldering iron with sandpaper.

TECHNIQUE
Brass Plant Stand

As well as soldering, this project uses brass tubing and rod which is very useful in making miniatures. It comes in 12in (305mm) lengths and is available from the Suppliers listed on page 146. Tubes,

BRASS PLANT STAND.

of course, are hollow and rods solid. Both are available in brass and copper.

The pot holders are made from brass jeans-style buttons. No need to cut them off your jeans; look for them in your local charity shop's button box. You can use any buttons, but they must be metal if you intend to solder them in place. (Alternatively, glue on plastic ones.)

I have given measurements for my plant stand as a guide, but you need not copy the measurements exactly. Sometimes following exact measurements can be more trouble, but no more effective, than judging by eye. If the proportions look about right, it will be fine.

METHOD

Bending the arms

1. Bend a small circular crook in the end of one of the ¾₆in (1mm) brass

Materials

- ⅛in (3mm) brass tube
- ¾₄in (1mm) brass rods x 4
- Brass buttons x 3
- Flux
- Solder
- Toothbrush
- Toothpaste
- Spray paint: gold
- Clear spray lacquer
- Potted plants x 3

rods, with thin-nosed pliers.

2 About ½in (13mm) from this, bend a circle in the rod.

3 Snip through the rod another ½in (13mm) along, so that this arm assembly is about 1½in (38mm) long.

4 Bend the other end of the arm into a slight curve.

5 Make two more identical arms from ¾₄in (1mm) brass rod.

Soldering the pot holders

1 Plug in the soldering iron.

2 Wash and dry the buttons.

3 Clean the base of the buttons and the ends of the arms with wire wool or a clean scouring pad.

4 Place a button upside-down on a wooden board. Apply a little flux to its centre, between the thread holes, and a little to the end of the brass rod arm.

TIP

KEEP THE PLIERS' JAWS CLOSED WITH AN ELASTIC BAND SO THAT YOU DON'T HAVE TO WORRY ABOUT LOOSENING YOUR GRIP.

5 Grasp the arm with pliers.

6 Dip the tip of the soldering iron into the flux. If it sizzles, it's ready.

7 Touch the tip of the iron to the solder, and hold it there until some solder melts onto it.

8 Rest the end of the arm over the centre of the button.

Fig 5.15 Soldering the brass arm to the button.

9 Touch the tinned tip of the soldering iron to the arm. Hold this position while the arm and button heat to the required temperature. When this happens, the solder will quickly melt and run into the joint. Apply enough solder to make a solid joint, but not too much as this will appear lumpy. (Alternatively, you can deposit some solder on the button and press the arm into it. If you work this way you'll need to heat the arm up too, by placing the iron on top of it.)

10 Remove the soldering iron and allow the assembly to cool for several minutes.

Fig 5.16 Soldering the plant holders to the central tube.

SOLDERING

- To make a good joint, both surfaces *must* be clean and not tarnished.
- When you are soldering elsewhere on the assembly, previously soldered joints may become unsoldered if they get heated by conduction from the iron. If you have trouble with this, bind the soldered joints together tightly with fuse wire. Remove the wire once the solder is solid again. (You can also solder fuse wire into the joint, so long as it's clean and fluxed.)
- Ideally, apply as little solder as possible. The less solder applied, the less obtrusive it is, but don't get too fussy; if it's joined, that's good enough.
- Lumpy joints can be sanded down once cool.
- To unsolder a joint, reheat it with the iron to melt the solder.
- Self-fluxing solder is also available to make the job even more straightforward.
- Brass solder is available, but it's expensive. You can give your silver solder a coat of brass paint to blend it in if you feel it's obtrusive.

Fig 5.17 Applying solder to the base of the stand.

Safety

♦ A plugged-in soldering iron can look deceptively cool! These irons get *very* hot. It is easy to forget this, particularly if you are new to soldering, and this could result in a nasty burn. My advice is: wear old leather gloves when handling the iron. This makes working slightly more awkward, but much less risky.

♦ Allow the soldering iron plenty of time to cool before attempting to move it or put it away.

♦ Remember that for several minutes, all metal parts that have been heated by the iron will be equally hot to the touch.

♦ Solder can splash. Always wear eye protection such as goggles.

♦ Soldering is not suitable for unsupervised children.

♦ Work on an old wooden board. The soldering iron will very quickly burn through a work surface. A chopstick rest makes a good soldering iron rest, or improvise with the likes of a small tin of tomato purée.

⓫ Once cool, test the joint for strength by gently wiggling it.

⓬ Repeat for the remaining two arms and buttons.

> **TIP**
>
> DON'T WORRY IF THE BUTTONS AREN'T ALL HORIZONTAL. A CERTAIN AMOUNT OF CAREFUL ADJUSTMENT CAN BE MADE WITH PLIERS ONCE THE STAND IS SOLDERED.

The stand

❶ Cut a length of ⅛in (3mm) brass tube to measure ⁵⁄₁₆in (8mm), with a junior hacksaw.

❷ Using the above method, solder the three arms onto the stand at graduated heights, evenly spaced round the tube.

❸ Cut three 5in (127mm) lengths of ¹⁄₁₆in (1mm) brass rod.

❹ Bend a crook shape into one end of

> **TIP**
>
> BECAUSE THE JOINTS ARE SO CLOSE TOGETHER, THE FIRST JOINT MAY MELT AS YOU MAKE THE SECOND. IF THIS HAPPENS, SECURE THE SOLDERED JOINTS BY BINDING FIRMLY WITH FUSE WIRE. REMOVE THE WIRE WHEN COOL.

all three rods, with thin-nosed pliers.

❺ Thread the straight ends of all three rods into the central column of the plant stand, with the crooks at the top.

❻ Adjust the crooks at the top to graduate in height, and space them evenly.

❼ Trim at the straight ends to an even length.

❽ Bend out the ends at the base so that they splay into level feet, and then bend a crook shape into the end of each foot.

❾ Apply a little solder into the base of the central column to secure the feet and hold them in position.

❿ Carefully bend the arms of the stand to a uniform angle, using pliers, so that the pot shelves are horizontal.

Finishing

❶ Polish the stand with an old toothbrush and toothpaste. Rinse well and dry.

❷ Paint the solder gold and set aside to dry.

❸ Spray the entire assembly with clear lacquer to prevent tarnish.

❹ Secure pot plants into the button holders with Gripwax. (Gripwax does a similar job to Blu-tack, but is less obtrusive and so is ideal for miniature work.)

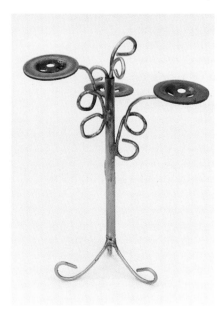

Fig 5.18 The stand sprayed with clear lacquer.

CHAPTER SIX

Wooden Furnishings

Wooden Furnishings

A good selection of wood sheets, strips, moulding and turned banister spindles is invaluable to the dolls' house DIY-er. They are available from dolls' house and craft shops or mail order and are useful for constructing simple pieces of wooden furniture and small accessories. Practically no woodwork is required if you make the best use of wood sheet and strip.

Don't worry too much about colour: most wood can be stained to resemble any other wood, but dark wood cannot be 'stained' lighter and wood stain cannot easily be removed once it has soaked in. Wood grains such as oak, although authentic, are too large to look right in miniature. Many miniaturists prefer to use a substitute such as sweet chestnut. More exotic-sounding wood sheets, which are easy to work with and finish because of their fine texture, are readily available. Jelutong, from Malaya, can be stained to resemble other woods. Basswood (lime) is European and one of the 'harder' softwoods. Obeche (a hardwood from Cameroon) and ramin (a hardwood from Sarawak) are also popular, but are becoming endangered because of this.

If the wood is to be painted or upholstered, I often recycle wooden vegetable crates or old drawer bottoms. Use a specialist wood glue. This will give a strong, rigid bond, but it is comparatively slow to dry. A project can be speeded up by using a rapid drying epoxy resin such as Araldite Rapid. Always wipe away any excess glue before it dries. Dried-on glue looks unsightly, and wood stain cannot penetrate it.

TECHNIQUE
Using Moulding

Specialist wooden mouldings and turnings are intended for making cornices, skirting, staircases and balconies, but can easily be adapted to make simple furniture. This is a good way to begin woodworking as no skills are needed and the results are practically instant.

PROJECT
Pedestal Tables

These pedestal tables involve *no* woodwork. They are made from thin chunks of cornice, turned balusters and wooden badge mounts. The latter are available in packs of different shapes and sizes from craft shops. These tables are very useful since they fit in with practically any setting and can be decorated to complement any period.

This project also touches on miniature ceramic tiling. Miniature tiles are used in exactly the same way as

PEDESTAL TABLES.

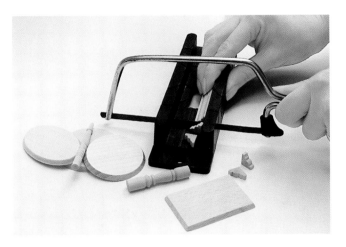

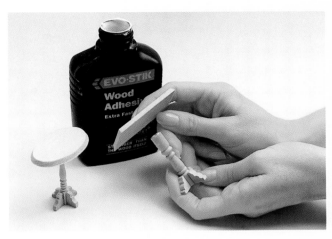

ABOVE LEFT: *Fig 6.1 Cutting sections of cornice.*

ABOVE: *Fig 6.2 Gluing the badge mount to the baluster.*

full-size tiles, but their thickness can make them look out of scale. This can be remedied by fitting them into a recess. The tiny tiles used in the full-size craft of mosaic tiling can be used by miniaturists. Sheets of these sometimes turn up in charity shops. Swimming pool tiles can also be used. (Specialist swimming pool shops sometimes have bags of mixed tiles.) An alternative to using ceramic tiles is to paint a product such as Dimensional Magic onto printed tiles. This gives a very realistic 3-D tiled effect.

METHOD

Pedestal table

1 Cut four matching ⅛in (3mm) slices from the cornice off-cut with a junior hacksaw and a mitre block.

2 Glue the four cornice slices at right-angles to one end of the baluster to form the pedestal. Set aside to dry. (If using a banister spindle, glue the cornice slices to the thicker end.)

TIP

IF YOU INTEND TO STAIN THE WOOD, EITHER STAIN BEFORE GLUING OR WIPE ANY EXCESS GLUE FROM THE WOOD BEFORE IT DRIES.

3 Glue the badge mount to the top of the pedestal. (If you use a banister

Materials
Pedestal and painted tables

◆ Baluster OR banister spindle and flat wooden bead
◆ Off-cuts of large cornice
◆ Wooden badge mount
◆ Fine sandpaper
◆ Wood glue
◆ Wood stain
◆ French polish OR emulsion paint: off-white
◆ Acrylic paint: blue

Tiled table

◆ Scrap of wood sheet
◆ Blu-tack
◆ Mosaic tiles x 9
◆ Off-cut of dado rail or similar
◆ Superglue
◆ 4 square-topped banister spindles
◆ ⅛in (3mm) square wood strip
◆ Spray primer: white
◆ Polyfilla
◆ Acrylic paint: blue

spindle, glue a flat wooden bead to the pointed end of the banister spindle to increase the surface area, then glue the bead to the badge mount.)

4 Once dry, sand the base of the table flat so that the cornice slices are even and the table stands level.

5 Stain the table with wood stain and

KNOW-HOW
MOULDINGS

◆ Turnings can be customized for a particular use. Cut a section from the length or trim it down from one end.

◆ Glue repels wood stain so it's often a good idea to stain mouldings and turnings before you glue them.

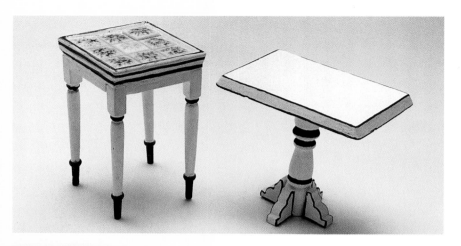

Fig 6.3 The tables painted in white with detail picked out in blue.

the dado strips in place around the tile block. Set aside to dry.

3 When dry, remove the tiles from the dado frame.

4 Cut the empty dado frame away from the wood sheet to make the table top.

5 Trim down the banister spindles if they look a little long for table legs. I cut ⅜in (10mm) off mine.

6 Glue one banister under each corner of the table.

7 Measure and cut to size thin wood strip stretchers to fit between the legs. Glue the stretchers in place.

8 Spray the assembly with a couple of coats of white spray primer and set aside to dry.

9 Glue the tiles back into the dado frame.

10 Wipe a little Polyfilla or plaster over the tiles to grout (fill in the gaps).

11 Pick out the detail in blue acrylic paint.

ALL SORTS OF SIMPLE FURNITURE CAN BE PUT TOGETHER THIS WAY. KITCHEN FURNITURE IS PARTICULARLY EFFECTIVE. TRY A SIMPLE KITCHEN TABLE, THEN STOOLS AND CHAIRS AND EVEN SHELVING MADE FROM READY-CUT WOOD SHAPES AND READY-TURNED BANISTER SPINDLES.

apply a coat of french polish or paint with a coat of off-white emulsion.

Painted table

1 Decorate the painted table by picking out the detail with acrylic paint (see photo of completed tables).

Tiled table

1 Blu-tack the nine tiles to a corner of the uncut wood sheet.

2 Edge the tile block with the dado strip, mitreing the edges neatly. Glue

Routing technique

1 It helps to drill four pilot holes, two at the top of the recess and two at the bottom, to start the rout.

2 Place the routing tool in the holes and gently pare away the wood until you reach the opposite holes.

3 Compare the slat to the recess as you work. Rout out sufficient wood to accommodate the slat.

4 Smooth the finished recess by gently stroking the router along the sides.

TECHNIQUE

Routing

Routing is a woodworking term meaning gouging out a recess or channel. It is useful for creating strong wooden joints where one piece fits into another, as for the slats on a bedstead. It can be done by hand or machine. If you have a mini power drill, you can buy a specialist routing bit. Routing by hand is not difficult, just more laborious.

PROJECT

Georgian Four-Poster Bed

I am not a skilled woodworker. Actually, I'm not any sort of woodworker. However, that does not stop me contriving convincing-looking wooden furniture. This project makes use of ready-made turned veranda posts and plain wood strip and sheet. (Lathe turning is a challenge I have never attempted because turned wooden hardware is readily available from dolls' house suppliers.)

The sizes of the wood strips are

arbitrary. They just happened to be what came to hand. It will make no difference to the end result if your wood strips or sheet measure slightly more or less than mine. Either wood glue or epoxy resin will glue the frame together, but epoxy resin is quicker.

I decorated the front of the bed frame with a strip of fancy beading. The paint finish is achieved with several thin coats of off-white car spray paint. 'Volkswagen Pastel White' is ideal for a soft, antique white finish.

The drapes are made from full-size upholstery trim and an old silk neck scarf (which has more fabric than a headscarf) from a charity shop. The back and canopy are decorated with pleated silk mounted on thin cardboard. I used spray starch to achieve an authentic draped effect. The blanket is a blue duster.

GEORGIAN FOUR-POSTER BED.

METHOD

Frame construction

1 Shorten the veranda posts so that one end measures 2in (51mm) down from the first turn and the overall length is 8in (203mm). These are the 'front bedposts'.

2 Cut two 8in (203mm) 'back bed-posts' from the ⁹⁄₁₆ x ⅜in (14 x 10mm) wood strip.

3 Cut two 7in (178mm) 'side struts' from the ⅞ x ³⁄₁₆in (22 x 5mm) wood strip.

Fig 6.4 Marking out, drilling and routing the back bedposts.

Materials

Bed

- Wooden veranda posts x 2 (for front posts)
- ⅞ x ³⁄₁₆in (22 x 5mm) wood strip (for side and front bed struts)
- ⁹⁄₁₆ x ⅜in (14 x 10mm) wood strip (for back posts)
- 7¹¹⁄₁₆ x 5¾in (195 x 146mm) wood sheet (for back panel)
- Large cornice
- ⅛in (3mm) dowel
- Decorative beading
- Wood glue or epoxy resin
- Spray primer: white
- Spray paint: white (e.g. Volkswagen Pastel White)

Drapery

- Thin cardboard
- Tacky glue
- Upholstery trim
- ⅛in (3mm) dowel
- Silk
- Spray starch

ROUTING

- To rout by hand, gouge out the bulk of the recess with a craft knife and finish with a router (you can improvise with a drill bit).
- Practise on a scrap of spare wood before venturing onto the project.
- If you accidentally rout out too much wood, pack the hole with wood filler after you make the join.

Safety

When routing with a power drill, it is very easy to slip. Routing bits are very vicious, more so than drill bits, so always wear thick protective gloves and eye protection. (I took my gloves off for the photos in order to give a clearer picture.)

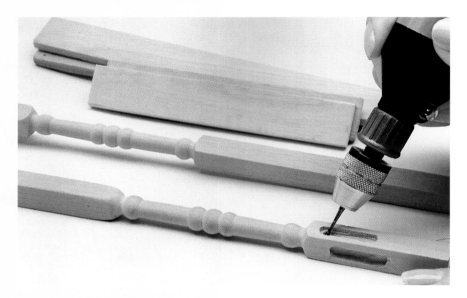

Fig 6.5 Routing the second holes on the front bedposts.

BELOW: *Fig 6.6 The bed components assembled.*

BELOW RIGHT: *Fig 6.7 The bed primed and sprayed off-white.*

④ Cut one 5⅛in (130mm) 'front strut' from the ⅞ x 3⁄16in (22 x 5mm) wood strip.

⑤ On one side of both the lower halves of the front bedposts, mark a line in pencil, 1in (25mm) up from the base, in the centre of the post. These lines indicate the position of the side struts. Place the base of the side strut on this line, ensure that it is positioned centrally on the post, and trace around it.

⑥ Mark on similar lines to indicate the position of the strut holes, 1in (25mm) up from the base of the back bedposts.

⑦ Rout out these marked areas so that the side strut fits snugly into the slots in the front and back bedposts, but don't glue yet.

⑧ On an adjacent side of the front bedposts, mark a second area to be routed, ⅞in (22mm) up from the base. Be sure you make a left- and a right-hand post so that these lower slots face each other and the higher slots face the front. The lower slots will take the front strut.

⑨ Rout out the slots to take the front struts.

⑩ Glue one back bedpost to each long side of the wood sheet back panel. The back panel should end ⅜in (10mm) up from the base of the post. Set aside to dry.

Assembly

① Fit the front strut into the lower slots, but do not glue yet.

② Glue the side struts into the higher

slots on the front and back bedposts.

3 Now glue the front strut into place. Set aside to dry.

TIP

USE ELASTIC BANDS TO KEEP THE STRUCTURE SQUARE AS THE GLUE DRIES.

4 Cut three lengths of cornice to fit round the top of the bed frame. Mitre the corners with a mitre block.

TIP

DOUBLE-CHECK THE POSITION BEFORE CUTTING THE MITRE AND ENSURE THEY ARE ALL CUT THE SAME WAY UP AT THE APPROPRIATE ANGLE.

5 Glue the cornice round the top of the bed frame. Hold in place with elastic bands and set aside to dry.

6 Glue the decorative beading to the front of the front strut.

Painting

1 Spray the bed frame with a couple of coats of white spray primer.

2 Spray with several thin coats of 'Volkswagen Pastel White' spray paint.

Pleated headboard

1 Cut a piece of thin cardboard to fit the headboard of the bed frame.

2 Cut a rectangle of silk a little longer and twice as wide as the cardboard headboard.

3 Glue one edge to the back of the long side of the cardboard. Pleat the silk nearest the edge onto itself to make a small tuck. Pin this tuck in place at both ends. Pleat and pin a second tuck next to the first in the same way. Continue to pleat and pin the silk until you reach the opposite side. Glue the free end onto the back of the cardboard.

4 Glue the pleated and pinned over-lap over the top and bottom of the cardboard to keep the pleats in place.

5 Secure the 'pleated card' to the headboard with a few dots of glue.

Pleated canopy

1 Cut a thin piece of cardboard to fit the canopy of the bed frame.

2 Cut a length of silk about 20 x 5in (508 x 127mm) for the canopy.

3 Gather one of the long edges with running stitch and tie it tightly into a bunch. Sew through the bunch to

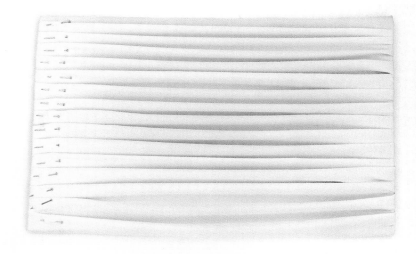

Fig 6.8 The pleated headboard decoration.

Fig 6.9 The pleated canopy decoration.

Fig 6.10
Fitting the drapes.

6 Glue the fabric overlap onto the back of the cardboard. The back won't be visible once it's in the room setting, but if you like, glue a section of silk over the back of the cardboard to neaten its appearance.

7 Fit the pleated cardboard canopy into the top of the bed frame.

Drapes

1 Cut two lengths of dowel to fit between the front and back posts, a little long so they wedge into place.

2 Cut two 8in (203mm) squares of silk to make the drapes.

3 Hem three sides of each piece. These will be the front, base and back edges. (I also trimmed the front edge with some cord from the upholstery trim.)

4 Sew a large hem along the remaining top edge.

5 Thread this top hem onto the dowel and wedge the dowel between the back and front posts.

6 Trim the fringe of the upholstery trim to a suitable length and glue it round the outside edge of the canopy.

7 Glue a curtain tie to each back post. (I plaited some cord from the upholstery trim.)

8 Spray the curtains liberally with spray starch, gather them back, and tie them to the back posts with the curtain tie. Arrange the curtains attractively.

VARIATIONS

VARIOUS STYLES OF FOUR-POSTER BEDS CAN BE MADE THIS WAY. FOR A VICTORIAN FOUR-POSTER, TRY A STAINED AND FRENCH POLISHED FINISH. EACH BED CAN LOOK VERY DIFFERENT ACCORDING TO YOUR CHOICE OF WOOD FINISH AND DECORATION. THICK WOODEN PAINT BRUSH HANDLES CAN BE USED FOR PLAINER END POSTS.

secure it very firmly. There will be some pull on this area which will be the central point of the canopy.

4 Glue the back of this gathered bunch to the centre of the cardboard canopy with tacky glue. Set aside to dry.

5 When dry, allow the fabric to fall over the cardboard and pin it into regular tuck pleats. Pull the fabric fairly tightly to create a swirl coming from the centre.

TECHNIQUE

French Polishing

This technique isn't true french polishing, it's just my own way of finishing wood furniture. I first began to experiment with polish because I was dissatisfied with the finish on cheap imported furniture. In my opinion, french polish gives a much better finish to miniature furniture than regular varnish.

Even the lowliest of imported

furniture can be given an antique finish that gives the impression that it's far worthier. It's not difficult. It does involve a little time and effort, but not as much as having to make the piece from scratch.

French polish is a shellac-based varnish which can be bought from any hardware store. Button polish (made from 'buttons' of shellac) is similar and used in the same way as french polish, but gives a harder, more orange finish. Personally, I prefer french polish. French polish differs from varnish in that it will not repel water. This shouldn't be a problem in the dolls' house environment, unless the miniature inhabitants are very careless with their coffee mugs.

The other difference between french polish and varnish is that it dries in about 15 minutes. This may sound like an advantage, and it is to some degree, but it also means that a slightly different application technique is required for french polish than for standard varnish. You can apply as many coats of french polish as you like. One coat will give a dull sheen, several coats will give a high gloss finish. Simply stop when your desired effect has been achieved. Coats of french polish should not be allowed to harden completely between applications. Several thin coats give a much better finish than one thick one. Leave the polish to harden for 24 hours once all the coats have been applied.

PROJECT
French-Polished Long-Case Clock

Long-case (grandfather) clocks are fun to customize. Changing the clock face and the innards goes a long way to working the transformation. You can use a suitable picture clipping from a catalogue. Be sure to choose a clipping that is photographed straight on. A distorted clock face will not look convincing. Add wristwatch hands to the dial for added authenticity.

I have 'french polished' many pieces of furniture, but this long-case clock was quite a challenge since it was really grotty in its original state. I dressed it with proprietary marquetry banding and added two 'square twisted plainhead' nails to the clock face case. This decoration is optional, depending on whether the look will suit your clock, but the concept remains the same. Non-wood decorations can be incorporated into wooden furnishings, providing they are carefully painted to blend in with the wooden structure and polished along with the rest.

METHOD

French polishing
1 Remove and discard the clock door handle, the clock face and the pendulum.

FRENCH-POLISHED LONG-CASE CLOCK.

2 Apply paint stripper thickly all over the clock. Leave for about 10 minutes to soak in, then begin to scrub off the varnish with an old toothbrush. Apply

Stripping technique
To french polish a piece of cheap furniture, it is necessary to strip the original varnish. Any brand of paint stripper will do.

1 Remove handles, trim and any acetate glazing before applying the stripper.

2 Disassemble the piece as much as possible. Remove drawers and doors. Separate pieces are easier to work on.

3 Using an old paint brush, cover the furniture with a liberal coat of paint stripper. Work the stripper well into the varnish. Paint stripper takes about 15 minutes to work. Keep applying more stripper if the surface dries.

4 After about 10 minutes, the surface varnish will begin to lift and bubble. Scrub away the varnish with an old toothbrush. Apply more stripper as necessary, scrubbing all over the piece, but paying particular attention to corners and edges.

5 Leave the stripper to act for a further 10 minutes or so, then scrub it off with an old kitchen scourer. Leave the piece to dry off in the open air for a few hours.

6 Wipe the piece over with white spirit. (Actually, I use surgical spirit because I can't stand the smell of white spirit.) This serves two purposes: it removes any stripper residue and also shows up any areas of remaining varnish as shiny patches. If necessary, repeat the stripping process a second time. It's best to remove as much varnish as possible during the stripping stage as this cuts down on the hard work of sanding.

7 If your piece falls apart because the stripper dissolves the glue, don't worry – it's often easier to strip the individual pieces, but remember how all the pieces fit together. It is fine to clean off the glue, but don't sand the joint. The pieces won't fit together so well if the edges are rounded off.

RIGHT: *Fig 6.11*
The original long-case clock.

FAR RIGHT: *Fig 6.12*
The clock stripped and sanded.

KNOW-HOW
SANDING

◆ Never be tempted to use a coarse sandpaper on miniature furniture. This will cause deep scratches which are difficult to erase and which spoil the finished effect. Use as fine a grade of sandpaper as possible for the job.

◆ Always sand along the grain.

◆ Use a sanding block (sandpaper wrapped round a small wooden block) to sand along edges so as not to round them off.

◆ Use a piece of folded sandpaper to sand into edges and corners.

◆ When you feel you have achieved a smooth enough finish, wipe over the piece with white spirit to remove the sanding dust and check that no varnish remains. If you go on to the next step with remnants of old varnish, the end result will be patchy and disappointing.

Materials

◆ Long-case clock
◆ Paint stripper
◆ White spirit
◆ Wood stain
◆ French polish
◆ Old toothbrush
◆ Sandpaper
◆ Twisted nails x 2 (optional)
◆ Acrylic paint: to tone with clock case
◆ Clock face clipping
◆ Wristwatch hands
◆ Snippet of Butyrate or acetate sheet
◆ Marquetry banding (optional)
◆ Medium brass chain
◆ Brass end caps x 2
◆ Cocktail stick
◆ Small brass shank button
◆ Scrap of wood strip
◆ Brass door handle

more paint stripper as it dries. Repeat if necessary until all the varnish is removed. Set aside to dry.

3 Sand the clock case with fine sandpaper to remove any stubborn varnish and to smooth the grain. Don't forget to sand inside the case too.

4 Wipe over with white spirit to remove the sanding dust.

5 Apply a coat of wood stain. (I used Georgian Light Oak for this project.) Set aside to dry.

Safety

◆ Wear thick gloves and eye protection to avoid damage from splashes of stripper.

◆ Protect the work surface from the stripper with newspaper.

◆ Work in a well-ventilated atmosphere, preferably outside.

FRENCH POLISHING

♦ You can apply the polish with a 'rubber'. To make a rubber, wrap a piece of cloth over a small piece of cotton wool. Apply a little polish to the rubber and rub this over the wood in a circular motion for the initial coats. Apply the last coat with straight strokes.

♦ The rubber can sometimes stick, so french polishers apply a spot of oil to the rubber to help it glide. Traditionally, linseed oil is used, but any vegetable oil will do.

♦ If your french polish becomes too thick to work with, thin it carefully with a little methylated spirit.

♦ You can also apply french polish more simply with a paint brush, working systematically over the piece. Brush the polish on thinly, working quickly to prevent the brush hairs sticking to the polish and spoiling the sheen. As soon as the first coat feels dry but tacky (this only takes a few minutes), start to apply the next coat.

♦ Since french polish is solvent-based, clean brushes with white spirit.

♦ A useful time-saving tip on brush cleaning (which everyone hates) is to clean out an old nail polish bottle with acetone, then fill the bottle with french polish. This gives you a handy bottle of french polish complete with application brush which never needs cleaning. It's useful to have similar bottles of wood stains. Keep them handy and refill when necessary. (To fill a small-necked bottle, dribble the liquid down an orangewood stick.)

♦ French polish is very sticky. It can practically be used as glue. This means that if you don't wipe the bottle top before screwing on the lid, you'll probably never get it off again! If this should happen, try wrapping a thick elastic band round the lid and twisting it off while wearing a rubber glove. If it's really stuck, run the bottle top under the hot tap first. This technique can be used to undo practically any stubborn lid.

♦ If you fancy trying some variations to traditional french polish, white polish is bleached transparent, button polish is more orange, garnet polish is dark brown and black polish gives an ebony finish.

6 At this stage I added some marquetry banding on either side of the case and a large twisted nail on either side of the clock face. I drilled two small holes in the upper part of the clock to accommodate the nail ends. Before fitting, I painted the nails brown, to tone in with the wooden case.

7 Apply three or four thin coats of french polish, allowing the polish to become tacky between coats. Coat the nails with french polish to help them blend in with the clock case.

Decorating

1 Mount the clock face clipping on thin card. Carefully glue the wristwatch hands over the original hands, with superglue.

2 Glue the clock face in place on the clock.

3 Cut and fit a piece of Butyrate or acetate sheet over the clock face to stand for glass.

4 Fit the end caps to the ends of a

STAINING

♦ The ready-made furniture we are working with is often already stained. It is practically impossible to remove wood stain, so the stain you choose will need to be similar in tone or darker than the original. Choose pale, unstained furniture to strip if you want a free hand in choosing the colour of the stain.

♦ Coat the piece evenly with wood stain. Allow to dry.

♦ Apply a second coat of stain if you want a deeper colour.

♦ If you use a solvent-based stain, you can save on brush cleaning by using a disposable cotton bud to apply the stain. Be sure to brush away any fluff from the cotton bud before applying it.

♦ Water-based wood stains are also available.

RIGHT: *Fig 6.13 The stained clock.*

FAR RIGHT: *Fig 6.14 Adding marquetry banding and several coats of french polish.*

length of medium chain for weights.

5 Trim and stain the cocktail stick, then fit the shank of the button to the end of it to make a pendulum.

6 Glue the weights and pendulum to a scrap of wood strip, then glue this assembly inside the clock case.

7 Fit a replacement brass handle to the clock case door.

VARIATIONS

YOU CAN MOUNT A FOB WATCH OR A WRISTWATCH MINUS THE STRAP IN PLACE OF THE ORIGINAL FACE. SUITABLE OLD WATCHES CAN BE PICKED UP VERY CHEAPLY IN SECOND-HAND MARKETS. UNLESS IT IS BATTERY RUN, YOU'LL NEED TO WIND IT EVERY DAY IF YOU WANT IT TO KEEP TIME!

Fig 6.15 Fitting the clock face, hands and glazing.

TECHNIQUE

Marquetry

Even a complete beginner can make miniature marquetry. There's a lot to learn about marquetry, but don't worry, I shan't be telling you all, just enough to get a pleasing result. The craft entails fitting together cut pieces of thin wood veneer to form a pattern or picture. This is then glued onto furniture for decoration.

When veneering furniture, the object is to attach it so that the join is undetectable. The effect given is that the whole piece of timber is made from the more precious veneer wood. The thinnest type of wood veneer is needed for miniature marquetry work. The best sources are stockists of marquetry veneer kits. Hobby's Annual stocks a ½kg (1lb) pack of veneer off-cuts that should last you a lifetime. I have also picked up abandoned marquetry kits from charity shops and jumble sales.

Marquetry banding in 1/12 scale is also available, but you can make banding yourself using the marquetry technique.

PROJECT

Veneered Cabinet

I used a veneer which looked to me like walnut for the main body of this cabinet. The inlaid motif is the easiest marquetry motif to make – the diamond.

Once the cabinet was finished, I decided not to replace the handles, but added two tiny lock plates instead. These I made from a couple of fancy

VENEERED CABINET.

KNOW-HOW

MARQUETRY

- Any piece of furniture can be veneered.

- For precise results, it's imperative you work with a brand new craft knife blade. If it becomes blunt, you may even need to renew the blade halfway through the project.

- Some veneers, such as oak, aren't suitable for miniature work because their grain would appear out of scale. Choose veneer with a fine 'miniature' grain.

- The decorative pattern is called the motif.

- The motif is incorporated or inlaid into the veneer which is then glued onto the furniture.

- When making motifs, choose veneers of contrasting colours, otherwise the marquetry effect will be lost.

- If you want to be fussy, when you cut the veneer, hold the craft knife at a slight angle away from the rule so that the cut is straight rather than sloping or chamfered. Discard the portion with the chamfered edge as this won't give the best join.

- When cutting veneer, make several light cuts over the cutting line rather than one heavy one – this may splinter the veneer.

- If you press too hard when cutting you are more inclined to slip.

- Wear close-fitting, old leather gloves when using a craft knife.

- Cut the veneer on a flat surface: an old lino tile is ideal.

- Once the veneer is dry it should be lightly, but thoroughly sanded so there are no obvious demarcation lines.

- If you don't fancy making and inlaying the motif, simply cover the piece with veneer sheet. Veneering can transform an inauspicious piece of cheap wood furniture.

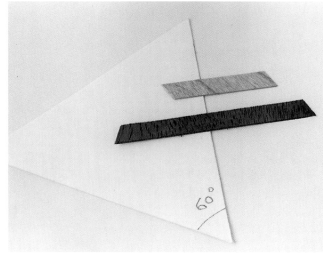

ABOVE: *Fig 6.16 The original cabinet.*

ABOVE RIGHT: *Fig 6.17 Cutting the veneer strips to a 60° angle.*

BELOW: *Fig 6.18 The four stages in making the diamond motif and fitting the diamond motif into the veneer.*

BELOW RIGHT: *Fig 6.19 Gluing the veneer to the sanded cabinet.*

chain links. Into one link I fitted a tasselled 'key', which is a tiny eyehook.

METHOD

Veneering the cabinet

1 Remove the cabinet's handles and make any other necessary modifications. (My cabinet needed a central wood strip added between the doors and, as veneer has to be glued to a flat surface, I also pared the raised panels off both doors, with a craft knife.)

2 Sand the cabinet to remove any varnish. Key (roughen) the door fronts, top and sides with coarse sandpaper. These areas will not be visible since

Materials

- ◆ Cheap wooden cabinet
- ◆ Sandpaper: medium and very fine
- ◆ Wood veneer sheets: light and dark
- ◆ Thick card
- ◆ Marquetry banding (optional)
- ◆ Fancy chain links x 2
- ◆ Tiny brass eyehook
- ◆ Silk cotton or embroidery thread
- ◆ Protractor
- ◆ French polish
- ◆ Superglue
- ◆ Wood glue

they will be covered with veneer.

③ Sand the base and legs smooth with fine grade sandpaper. These areas will remain uncovered.

④ Cut sections of veneer from the same sheet to fit the top, sides and doors.

⑤ Glue the top and side veneers, but not the doors, to the cabinet with wood glue. Be sure to cover the entire veneer with glue and press it on firmly until completely dry.

Making the motif

① Cut four lengths of veneer, all with a width of ³⁄₁₆in (5mm); two from a light wood veneer and two from a dark wood veneer. Their lengths don't matter, but their widths must match exactly.

② Cut one end of all the lengths to a 60° angle. (There is a mathematical reason why this angle has to be 60°, but we won't go into that.) The easiest way to do this is to measure and mark 60° onto the corner of a thick piece of card, using a protractor. Cut this angle out and use it as a template. Line up the base of the template with the edge of the strip and cut the angle with your craft knife. (If the grain splits, turn the strip the other way and try again.)

③ Smear a little wood glue onto a working surface (such as an old melamine chopping board). Place the two dark wood strips opposite each other, but flip one on its back. Lay them onto the glue with their points just touching (see Fig 6.18).

④ Turn the chopping board a quarter turn and do the same with the light wood strips, fitting them into the spaces created by the dark wood strips. You should have a pattern similar to a skewed cross (see Fig 6.18). Set aside to dry.

⑤ Once dry, carefully peel the motif from the chopping board. Lever it up with a craft knife if necessary. If it comes apart don't panic. Simply fit it together again backwards and place a few dots of superglue over any loose joins.

⑥ Using a steel rule, cut the ends off to make the diamond shape. Do this carefully and line up the last cut.

⑦ Cut a sliver of light wood veneer. Glue one edge of the diamond motif to the straight edge of the sliver with wood glue. Lay the diamond flat and allow to dry.

⑧ Once dry, cut the surplus wood from the sliver.

⑨ Trim one end of the sliver to continue the line of the diamond and repeat steps 7 and 8 on the next side.

ABOVE LEFT: *Fig 6.20 Fitting the marquetry banding.*

ABOVE: *Fig 6.21 French polishing the cabinet.*

SMALL ITEMS CAN BE MADE
ENTIRELY OF VENEER, FOR
EXAMPLE, TEA TRAYS, TEA
CADDIES, STATIONERY BOXES,
CHESSBOARDS AND DRAUGHTS-
BOARDS. FOR THESE, GLUE TWO
PIECES OF VENEER TOGETHER
TO MAKE THE MAIN BODY, THEN
INLAY TINY MOTIFS.

Fig 6.22 Fitting the locks, key and tassel.

🔟 Cover the diamond's two remaining
edges in a similar way and trim off the
excess.

⓫ Gently sand the back of the veneer
flat.

⓬ Make a second motif following the
same procedure.

Inlaying the motif

① Mark the mid-point on the width
and length of the door veneer, in
pencil.

② Line up the motif centrally and
carefully score round it.

③ Remove the motif, carefully cut out
the scored area and discard.

④ Smear the edges of the motif with
wood glue and fit it into the space in
the veneer. (Ensure it's the same way up
for a good fit.)

⑤ Glue the inlaid veneer panel to the
cabinet door.

⑥ Gently sand the surface smooth
with very fine grade sandpaper.

⑦ Repeat for the second door.

⑧ Cut and glue on the marquetry
banding.

Finishing

① Apply a couple of coats of french
polish to the cabinet.

② Carefully drill through the veneer
to the original holes for the door
handles. Find the site of the original
holes by probing with a pin.

③ Glue a fancy chain link over the
holes with superglue.

④ Attach a tiny tassel, made from silk
cotton or embroidery thread, to the eye
of the tiny eyehook.

⑤ Glue the eyehook point onto the
keyhole with superglue.

CHAPTER SEVEN

Using
Plastics

Using Plastics

Usually plastics are only appropriate in a modern setting. However, they do have legitimate
uses in the world of period dolls' houses. Coloured plastic sheeting makes attractive flooring
and clear plastic sheeting is the ideal material for glazing. Another invaluable plastic medium
is resin. This is used in the dolls' house world to simulate fluid.

PLASTIC SHEETING

- Plastic sheeting is best scored and snapped rather than cut with scissors as this gives a better line.
- Use tacky glue to fix plastic sheeting.
- To avoid pencil marks on the sheeting, mark out lines with a sharp T-pin instead. (This is just a large pin shaped like a T. The T-shape makes it easier to get a grip on than a regular pin.)

Using Plastic Sheeting

Thin plastic sheeting is ideal for making period or modern dolls' house flooring. (See Suppliers, page 146.) It can imitate marble, linoleum, floor tiles, wall tiles or vinyl flooring. The best thickness to use is 0.020in (0.5mm). It comes in a colour range of black, white, red, green, cream, blue, grey and brown.

Victorian Floor Tiles

Dolls' house floors are an important aspect of miniature décor. Even though flooring gets covered by rugs and fur-nishings, a suitable choice will enhance the overall effect of your room setting.

I chose green, cream, black and white sheeting to make up my Victorian floor tiles. Brown would also be an appropriate colour choice. The Victorians loved it, but I don't.

The tiles in this project are for a Victorian hall. Floor tiles are also suitable for landings, porches, conservatories, kitchens, servants' rooms and even grander downstairs rooms. Border patterns are a feature of this type of tiling. The border should differ slightly from the main pattern. As with all flooring, it is easiest to lay the tiles onto a false cardboard floor, than directly onto the dolls' house floor.

This project was made following metric measurements because I used a

VICTORIAN FLOOR TILES.

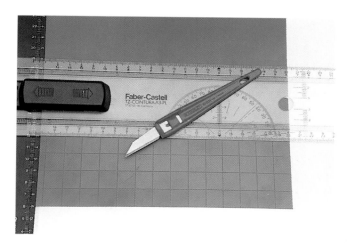

modern drawing board. When tiny variations in dimensions matter, accuracy can be easier in millimetres because they are smaller.

Materials

◆ 0.020in (0.5mm) plastic sheeting: cream, black, green and white
◆ Tacky glue
◆ Thin cardboard

METHOD

Cutting the tiles

1 Mark out ⅜in (10mm) square 'small'

tiles on all four plastic sheets, with a T-pin. (Quantities will depend on the size of the floor to be covered. Make a rough calculation before you begin and cut plenty.)

2 Press out one of the tiles and cut in half diagonally with a craft knife. Mark out the 'large' square tiles on the green sheet using the diagonal measurement of the small square. (The object is for the tiles to fit together. I've explained how I arrived at this measurement in case the size of your tile is slightly different from mine. My large tiles measure 1½in (38mm) square.)

3 Carefully score along all the

ABOVE LEFT: *Fig 7.1 Cutting the plastic tiles.*

ABOVE: *Fig 7.2 Laying the tiles along the central line.*

Fig 7.3 Half the floor completed.

VARIATIONS

VARIATIONS

TRY OUT YOUR OWN PATTERNS,
BUT BE SURE THEY TESSELLATE
BEFORE YOU BEGIN TO GLUE OR
YOU WILL BE LEFT WITH GAPS IN
YOUR TILING.

KNOW-HOW

TILE CUTTING

◆ Take time to mark out and cut each
strip of tiles accurately so that they
are all the same size and tessellate
(fit together). If individual tiles vary
too much, the resulting pattern will
be gappy and the pattern will go
awry towards the edges.

◆ Use a large set square or borrow a
drawing board to speed the cutting
process up and to improve accuracy.

◆ When scoring with a craft knife
and metal rule, your knife may slip
across the plastic. If this happens,
don't worry too much. Carry on
cutting the tile strips. When you
come to use the damaged strip, simply discard the spoilt tiles or use the
reverse side.

◆ As for full-size tiling, lay the first
tile in the centre. If you start from
the corner and work in, the pattern
becomes increasingly uneven.

◆ Smear small sections of the cardboard floor with a thin coat of
tacky glue and work outwards from
the centre.

◆ If your floor is asymmetrical like
mine, you will need to modify the
pattern to accommodate the border
pattern at the narrower width.

◆ Once the floor is in place, strips of
1/12 scale skirting fitted around the
wall edges will add greatly to the
finished effect.

Fig 7.4 The completed pattern.

pin lines using a sharp craft knife and
a straight edge. The drawing board I
borrowed for this project had a plastic
rule attached, but a steel rule is best:
it is easy to slice off bits of plastic rule
leaving you with an edge that is no
longer straight.

④ Score a diagonal line across three-
quarters of the black tiles, and all of the
white tiles.

⑤ Carefully snap the scored sheets
into strips, then snap the strips into
separate tiles.

Laying the tiles

① Measure the floor area and cut out
a false floor in thin cardboard.

TIP

THE EASIEST WAY TO DO THIS IS
TO MAKE A NEWSPAPER TEMPLATE;
THIS CUTS OUT ALL THE TIRESOME
MEASURING.

② Ensure that the cardboard base is
the right way up. Mark two bisecting
lines on the cardboard floor so that
they cross at the centre point.

③ Glue a black tile squarely over the
centre point.

④ Begin to lay the tiles, following the
pattern shown in the photos, from this
central point, along the bisecting pencil
lines, to form a cross-shape.

⑤ Tile all round the edge, following
the border pattern.

⑥ Fill in the rest of the pattern,
working from the centre out until you
meet the border. Try to keep the tiles
even, completing one section of pattern
at a time.

⑦ Once the entire card is tiled, place
the floor under a heavy book so that it
dries flat.

⑧ When dry, lightly rub over the
flooring with a soft eraser to remove
any gluey residue.

⑨ Turn the floor over and trim off
any overlapping tiles neatly with a
metal rule and craft knife.

TIP

DON'T WORRY IF THE TILED
SURFACE GETS GLUEY. IT'S EASIER
TO REMOVE ANY GLUE RESIDUE AT
THE END.

TECHNIQUE
Using Butyrate

A form of 'glass' is generally required, sooner or later, by all miniaturists. In miniature room settings full-size glass is generally too thick to be realistic. For the purist, ⅟₃₀in (0.8mm) glass is available, but glass this thin can prove problematic to work with. All forms of glass are very difficult for the amateur to cut to shape, not to mention a little lethal to fingers.

Many dolls' house kits come with thin acetate to glaze windows. I find acetate unsatisfactory because it is liable to bow, giving unnatural reflections in the windows. Clear Butyrate sheeting is an excellent alternative. It's ridged, cuts easily and (as long as the surface is not scratched), it imitates real glass exactly. Butyrate is not just useful for making windows; it is an excellent medium for making a conservatory, and for using in glass-fronted furniture or as glass shelving.

Thick Butyrate sheeting is sold in DIY centres as alternative glazing for greenhouses, but the ideal size for miniatures is a width of ⅟₂₅in (1mm) (available from *Hobby's Annual*). It comes with a thin blue protective film on both sides. This peels off to reveal crystal-clear 'glass'. Butyrate can be cut with a large pair of standard scissors, but it's easier to use power scissors. It can also be sawn, drilled and sanded.

PROJECT
Stained Glass Window

STAINED GLASS WINDOW.

Why stop at plain windows? Butyrate lends itself beautifully to creating a stained glass effect. The impression of lead is achieved using a proprietary liquid lead or relief outliner that comes in a squeezy bottle. There are several brands available in craft and hobby shops. None of them contain any real lead.

The 'glass' is coloured with specialist transparent tints. Tints can be blended together, just like regular paints. There are both spirit-based and water-based products available. Spirit-based tints give very professional results and are worth investing in if you think you might take up the hobby of glass painting. For miniature purposes, however, the water-based alternatives are adequate and more economical, as they are available in tiny pots on carded sets. Water-based glass tint is a viscous clear gel.

Fig 7.5 Pattern for stained glass window.

GLASS PAINTING

◆ If you are choosing your own design, small, complicated patterns are best avoided. Favour straight or gently curving lines, which are easier to reproduce in miniature.

◆ The squeezy bottle gives too thick a line for 1/12 scale work. Decant the liquid lead by squeezing some into a small clear bag. Twist the bag to force the liquid into the end and snip off the very tip with fine manicure scissors. The smaller the hole the better, as this gives a thinner line.

◆ Practise laying lines before you begin on the project. The technique is the same as piping icing from an icing bag.

◆ Start at the top of the pattern and work clockwise (anticlockwise if you are left-handed) so that your hand does not obscure or smudge your work. Turn the Butyrate sheet as you work for the same reason.

◆ Work with the bag resting on the surface. Squeeze and lay the liquid line slowly onto the Butyrate.

◆ Regularly wipe the tip of the 'piping bag' on kitchen paper to maintain a free-flowing line.

◆ Air bubbles or erratic squeezing may leave gaps. Don't worry about these. Once the design is finished, carefully fill in the gaps. After a moment or two, the lines will merge.

◆ Liquid lead lining takes about an hour to dry. If you are dissatisfied with the result, wipe off the lining immediately with kitchen paper, rinse the Butyrate in soapy water and have another go.

continued on page 77

METHOD

Lead lining

1 Cut the Butyrate to fit the window with a craft knife and metal rule.

2 Trace the stained glass window pattern given in Fig 7.5 or design your own.

3 Secure the Butyrate window over the stained-glass design with masking tape.

4 Fill a small plastic bag with liquid leading. Cut off the very tip of the bag to make a tiny piping bag.

Materials

◆ Butyrate sheeting
◆ Masking tape
◆ Liquid lead lining
◆ Glass paints

5 Begin by 'piping' the three circles. Add the straight lines, then fill in the rest of the pattern. (Follow the same order of curved lines, straight lines and

Fig 7.6 Tracing the pattern in liquid lead liner.

filling in for any designs.) Be careful not to smudge your work as you pipe.

6 Leave to dry for an hour.

Fig 7.7 Filling in the colour with glass paint.

Staining

1 Working with one colour at a time, carefully paint the tint into the sections created by the liquid leading. Set aside to dry.

continued from page 76

◆ If there are a few mistakes you would like to tidy once the design is dry, excess liquid lead can be carefully removed with the back of a craft knife (so that it doesn't scratch the Butyrate).

◆ Don't allow the glass tints to mix accidentally. Paint one colour at a time. Clean your brush thoroughly between colours.

◆ If using water-based tints, work with a dry brush so that you don't dilute the gel.

◆ Leave glass tints to dry overnight.

ALTERNATIVE MATERIALS

AN ALTERNATIVE TO LIQUID LEADING IS FULL-SIZE, SELF-ADHESIVE LEAD STRIP (AVAILABLE AT GLAZIERS AND DIY STORES). CUT THIS INTO THIN STRIPS WITH A CRAFT KNIFE AND METAL RULE SO THAT IT IS IN SCALE. LEAD STRIP WORKS BEST FOR DESIGNS MADE UP OF STRAIGHT LINES. REMEMBER LEAD IS POISONOUS. WASH YOUR HANDS THOROUGHLY AFTER CONTACT.

TECHNIQUE
Working with Resin

I was given a plastic embedding kit as a child. They don't seem to be available nowadays which is probably just as well because casting resin isn't really a suitable hobby for children. For adults, however, casting resin miniatures can be very rewarding, so long as you prepare well beforehand. Resin will give effects that can't be achieved in any other way.

Casting resin is a transparent syrup that comes in a tin. It needs a catalyst or hardener (peroxide) to cure it. The catalyst reacts chemically with the resin, heat is given off and the resin hardens. You can order resin by mail order or buy it in hobby shops. (Some shops don't stock it because it has a limited shelf life.)

Resin isn't difficult to use, but it's

sticky and rather smelly. To counteract these drawbacks, work in an outhouse if possible, be careful when pouring, and wear disposable gloves.

Resin can be tinted with translucent or opaque resin dyes to produce different colour 'liquids' such as orange juice, 'jelly' colours or 'formaldehyde' for medical specimens. Casting resin can be used in three ways:

◆ **To fill containers** Containers such as baths, basins, sinks and saucepans can be filled with resin. The resin resembles water which can contain accessories such as washing, vegetables or rubber ducks. The container should be regarded as permanently filled since it's practically impossible

Safety

◆ Resins should not be used by children unless under supervision.

◆ Use in a well-ventilated area, preferably outside.

◆ Anyone sensitive to volatile chemicals should wear a respirator.

◆ Wear disposable gloves.

◆ Resin can splash, so goggles are also a wise precaution.

◆ Be sure to dispose of all surplus resin safely. (Wrap in foil and put in an outside dustbin.)

◆ Resin and hardener are both highly flammable. Resin has a 'flash point' of 22–32°C (72–90°F).

STORING RESIN

◆ Resin has a limited shelf life; only four to six months even when stored in accordance with the manufacturer's instructions. It will go off (set) more quickly in a warm environment. Buy a small can just before you intend to use it then make all your resin projects at the same time.

◆ Store both resin and hardener in a cool environment, but don't let them freeze as this will cause them to spoil. Make sure the resin is at room temperature when you use it.

◆ Protect the hardener from light as exposure will eventually destroy its effectiveness.

VARIATIONS

YOU MAY ALSO COME ACROSS OPAQUE CAST RESIN MODELS SUCH AS MARBLE OR STONE FIREPLACES AND STATUES. TO MAKE THIS TYPE OF CAST RESIN MODEL YOU NEED TO MIX A 'FILLER POWDER', SUCH AS 'MARBLE FILLER POWDER', INTO A POLYESTER RESIN SUCH AS SUPERPOL. YOU THEN NEED TO MAKE A LATEX MOULD OF AN ORIGINAL (WHICH YOU MAY HAVE CARVED OR SCULPTED YOURSELF). THIS PROCESS IS MORE INVOLVED THAN THAT DESCRIBED ABOVE, BUT ONCE YOU HAVE YOUR MOULD, YOU CAN CAST AS MANY MODELS AS YOU LIKE. (REMEMBER NOT TO TAKE CASTS FROM OTHER PEOPLE'S WORK IF YOU WISH TO SELL THE MODELS, AS THEY OWN THE COPYRIGHT ON THE ORIGINAL DESIGN.)

to remove resin from ridged containers once it is cured.

◆ **To simulate liquid** Casting resin can be dribbled over accessories to simulate sauce or spilled liquid such as the albumin of raw eggs.

◆ **For casting** Solid castings can be cast in moulds. This technique is used when casting jellies, tureens, paperweights etc. Scour the house for sturdy, but flexible plastic lids to serve as moulds. If you use ridged metal moulds always use a 'mould release agent'. (I get by with a smear of light machine oil.) Remember that any undulation inside the mould will appear in reverse in your casting.

PROJECT
Cauldron of Irish Stew

A stew is an ideal resin project for the beginner because it doesn't matter if air bubbles become trapped in the casting. For this project you will need a large copper stop end as used in plumbing. Copper plumbing accessories make excellent miniature pots and pans. The stew ingredients are made from polymer clay. Instead of stew, the cauldron could hold jam, washing, gruel or anything boiling up.

You can suspend the stew ingredients in layers in the cauldron, but since I always fill the top layer with vegetables, the lower ones aren't visible. Now I simply fill the saucepan three-quarters full of resin and add just one layer of vegetables before topping up.

METHOD

Cauldron

① Drill a ⅛in (3mm) hole just below

CAULDRON OF IRISH STEW.

Materials

◆ 1³⁄₁₆in (30mm) copper stop end
◆ ³⁄₃₂in (2mm) copper rod
◆ Polymer clay (such as Fimo): green, yellow, grey, transparent, brown, orange and pink
◆ French polish
◆ Cocktail stick
◆ Sandpaper
◆ Casting resin
◆ Hardener
◆ Old newspaper or foil (to protect work surface)
◆ Clean, dry, disposable receptacles (e.g. yoghurt pot) x 3
◆ Clean, disposable stirrer (e.g. bamboo skewer)
◆ Clean, disposable dripper (e.g. cocktail stick)
◆ Plastic disposable syringe or plastic medicine measuring cup marked in millimetres
◆ Spray paint: black

the rim of the stop end. (Copper isn't as difficult to drill through as it looks.)
② Drill a second hole opposite the first hole.
③ Thread the copper rod through one of the holes and bend the end with thin-nosed pliers, so that it's fixed inside the pot.
④ Bend the handle round to the

Fig 7.8 Fitting the handle to the copper stop end.

Fig 7.9 Spraying the base with black spray paint.

opposite hole, thread the end through the hole and bend that end to fix it inside the pot. Snip off the excess rod with pliers.

⑤ Adjust the handle so that it looks symmetrical and even.

⑥ Spray the base of the cauldron with a squirt of black spray paint to simulate baked-on grease.

Stew ingredients

① To make carrots, blend a marble-sized ball of orange polymer clay with a peppercorn of yellow. Halve this ball and blend one half with an equal amount of transparent clay. Roll this into a matchstick-sized sausage. Flatten the remaining orange/yellow clay and wrap it round the sausage. Roll gently to 'blend', then chop slices from the sausage with a craft knife, leaving one end unsliced. From this end, carve a peeled carrot with a craft knife.

② Make slices of leek in the same way, but replace the orange Fimo with green. Before slicing, lightly score round the leek with the back of the craft knife to texture. Slice leaves in the uncut end with a craft knife.

③ To make potatoes, blend a scrap of yellow into a marble-sized ball of transparent Fimo. Carve a pea-sized potato shape from the ball by slicing off sections with a craft knife. Mix the bits into a ball again and carve out another potato. Make three potatoes and chop two into quarters. Press in a speck of brown here and there for 'eyes'.

④ To make the lamb cubes, lightly blend pea-sized balls of pink, grey, brown and transparent polymer clay. Press a few more specks of transparent clay onto the ball for fat. Roll into a sausage and square off the sides. Texture the sides by scoring with the back of a

continued on page 80

Fig 7.10 Stew ingredients made from Fimo.

KNOW-HOW
CASTING

◆ Dust can easily spoil your casting. Wipe all receptacles and utensils with spirit to ensure that they are free from fluff or dust.

◆ It is important to measure out the hardener very carefully: cure a film capsule of resin as a test to see how much hardener it requires.

◆ Mix the hardener into the resin slowly to avoid too many bubbles.

◆ Use the amount of hardener your product recommends, but I found the 1% mine recommended much too slow to cure. I used seven drops of hardener to every 10ml (2 tsp) of resin. (A 35mm film capsule filled just below the seal holds 30ml (6tsp), which weighs approximately 30g (1oz).)

◆ Ask at the chemist for a disposable syringe. These are very useful for measuring resin.

◆ If your casting gets very hot, warps or cracks, you've added too much hardener.

◆ If your casting doesn't set as quickly as you expect, you haven't added enough hardener, but don't discard it. Cover to prevent dust from settling on it and set aside for 24 hours or longer. Be patient, it will cure, eventually.

continued from page 79

TIP

ONCE HARDENED, POTATOES
CAN BE COATED WITH FRENCH
POLISH AND ROLLED IN ANY
BROWN POWDER, SUCH AS
COCOA, TO SIMULATE SOIL.

- Surgical spirit is the quickest way to clean resin from fingers and glassware.
- Like superglue, resin fogs plastic, so if you want to fill transparent receptacles, use only glass ones.
- Any object that doesn't contain moisture can be embedded in a casting. Moisture will cloud the resin.
- If you are embedding objects in different levels of resin in transparent receptacles and don't want a tell-tale demarcation line, don't allow the lower half of the resin to cure right through before adding the second layer.
- Proprietary resin dyes come in transparent and opaque shades. Blend the colour well into the resin before adding the catalyst. Water- or oil-based pigment will *not* tint resin. However, I have found that solvent-based tints, such as household varnish and some matt nail polishes, work reasonably well.
- Yoghurt pots or 35mm film capsules, when thoroughly clean and dry, make ideal disposable mixing pots.
- Bamboo skewers make good disposable stirrers.
- Toothpicks or cocktail sticks make useful drippers for hardener or tints.
- Use liquid detergent to rinse off any residual stickiness from your finished casting.

Fig 7.11 Filling the cauldron three-quarters full of resin.

Fig 7.12 Adding the stew ingredients and spoon handle, and topping up with resin.

craft knife. Cut the polymer clay roughly into cubes.

5 Harden the polymer clay stew ingredients in a cool oven, 100°C (200°F), for 10 minutes.

Wooden spoon

1 Round off the end of the cocktail stick with sandpaper.

2 Score a line ⅛in (3mm) down from the top of the spoon with a craft knife. Sand smooth. There's no need to worry about the spoon end since it will be stuck into the stew.

Adding the resin

1 Before you open the resin, get everything ready beforehand. Cover the work surface with newspaper. Set out two yoghurt pots, the bamboo skewer and the cocktail stick. Put on the disposable gloves and goggles and respirator if need be!

2 Open the tin or pierce the can top with scissors and pour some resin into one yoghurt pot. Replace the lid on the resin.

3 Draw up 5ml (1 tsp) of resin into the syringe and squirt this into the

second yoghurt pot.

4 Dip the cocktail stick into the hardener, allow 7–10 drops to drip into the resin, and stir with the bamboo skewer until thoroughly mixed.

5 Leave until the bubbles disperse, then slowly fill the cauldron three-quarters full.

6 Leave on a level surface, undisturbed, for 15 minutes.

7 After 15 minutes, check that the resin has gelled by gently tipping the cauldron. If it's still very runny, leave until it gels.

8 Once it has gelled sufficiently, carefully place the stew ingredients onto the gelled resin layer. Don't worry if some of it sinks a bit: this adds depth.

9 Stick the wooden spoon into the stew. Set aside to cure.

10 Mix up a second batch of resin as before in the third yoghurt pot. Pour this over the stew.

11 Wrap up the utensils well in plenty of newspaper and put into an outside dustbin.

12 Place the whole vegetables on a chopping board to complement the stew.

Soft Furnishings

Soft Furnishings

Cushions, quilts and upholstered furniture give a comfortable feel to a dolls' house. Proprietary soft furnishings are labour-intensive, which makes them expensive. However, since fabric is one of the easiest media to work with, it's very satisfying, and cost-effective, to make your own. Don't feel daunted if you're new to sewing. You don't have to be a skilled needleworker to get good results from miniature sewing; it's more important to be able to see your work clearly. (Work in a good light or with magnifying glasses.) A tiny running stitch is all that's required, though ambitious crafters might like to add backstitch to their miniature stitching repertoire.

Once you're used to wielding a needle, you will soon progress to upholstery. Miniaturists often find making furniture a challenge. Certainly, a degree of skill is required to make fine wooden miniatures. Fortunately for us, upholstered furniture is the exception. Cheap, upholstered furniture can be immeasurably improved by re-covering it in a luxurious fabric. There's a great deal of scope here for the amateur since anyone can upholster. It's simply a case of systematically wrapping fabric (or leather) round a wooden frame. The next step is to try your hand at making a loose cover for a chair and from there, to construct and cover your own furniture.

KNOW-HOW
LACE

- To thread thin ribbon through lace holes quickly, thread the ribbon through the eye of a darning needle and 'sew' it through.
- If the lace you find looks too white, you can antique it by soaking it briefly in weak black tea.
- It's not generally necessary to hem lace, but the ends can look a little ragged. To neaten, dampen the cut end with a little starch and roll it under. It should stay put neatly.

TECHNIQUE
Lace Trimming

Quality, lace-trimmed miniatures look opulent, but are not readily available commercially. However, lace is the easiest fabric to work with because it requires no hemming. As I hope you will agree from the following project, a rather commonplace cradle can soon be transformed into something very impressive.

The choice of lace makes all the difference. Where possible, use cotton lace; it drapes better and does not have a synthetic sheen. Cotton lace can be hard to track down nowadays so it's probably best not to go shopping specifically for old cotton lace, just buy it when you see it. Specialist miniature drapers do stock it, but a cheap and ready source is charity shops. Look out for 'Lace Events' or ask if they have a 'Lace Box'. Miniaturists can pick up tiny snippets for next-to-nothing because we're the only people who can use them.

Thin, synthetic ribbon is available from high street haberdashers, but silk ribbon gives a better effect because, being a natural fibre, it drapes much better. It's not expensive and it is well worth the extra effort of ordering it from a miniature supplier.

PROJECT

Lace Cradle

The cradle I used for this project came in a cheap boxed set. The method can easily be adapted to suit any cradle. It need not be left plain. It could be painted, french polished, distressed or decorated with transfers. If your cradle has no decorative knobs you could glue on some wooden beads or fix the ribbons to the sides. The only constraint is that the deep lace needs to be a similar depth to the cradle. The lace I used already had larger holes into which I could thread the ribbon, but since lace is inherently holey, it's usually no problem to choose a pattern of holes to thread the ribbon through.

Materials

◆ Cheap wooden cradle
◆ 7in (178mm) length of deep lace x 3
◆ 7in (178mm) length of narrow lace x 2
◆ Matching thread
◆ Spray starch
◆ Snippet of plain cotton fabric
◆ Snippet of foam
◆ 1¼yd (1.2m) thin ribbon
◆ ¹⁄₁₆in (1mm) brass rod

METHOD

Hood trim

1 Drill a ¹⁄₁₆in (1mm) hole in the centre of the head of the cradle.

2 Bend the end of the brass rod into a small loop, using pliers.

3 Bend a right angle into the rod

LACE CRADLE.

MINIATURE SEWING

◆ Thanks to the current revival of patchwork quilting, there is a good selection of small-print fabrics on sale. Most shops will sell a ¼yd (¼m) from the roll.

◆ Always work with clean hands. Natural oils from your fingers will soon make your miniature work grubby, particularly if it's white.

◆ Cheap sets of coloured spools of thread are invaluable to the miniaturist. They save buying a whole reel for every project. An added bonus is that the thread is generally very thin and therefore less obtrusive. Though more expensive, silk thread is also suitable.

◆ Use as fine a needle as you can work with to avoid unsightly needleholes in the fabric.

◆ Seams are often bulky, but sometimes necessary. Where possible, make use of the fabric's selvage (the machined edge) to avoid them.

◆ For the tiniest hem, dampen the edge of the fabric very slightly and roll it as tightly as you can until the frayed edge disappears. Flatten the roll and slip stitch along the wrong side. To work slip stitch, catch a thread of fabric from under the folded edge, then a thread of fabric from the seam. Repeat ⅛in (3mm) along for each subsequent stitch.

◆ A sewing machine can be used to make miniature soft furnishings but, with the exception of quilting, it doesn't save much time. It's difficult to sew slow enough and all too easy to 'miss-stitch'. Unpicked machine stitches look messy, but by all means have a go. Use thin thread, the finest needle, the shortest stitch length, and turn the machine by hand.

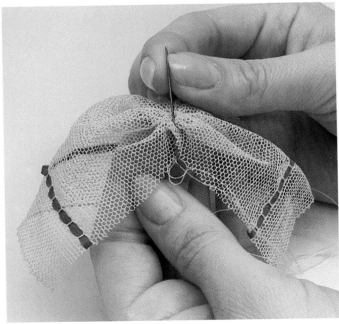

ABOVE: *Fig 8.1 Fitting the brass rod to the cradle.*

ABOVE RIGHT: *Fig 8.2 Sewing the hood trim.*

A FOUR-POSTER BED OR DRESSING TABLE CAN BE TRANSFORMED INTO A ROMANTIC CREATION WITH LACE AND SILK RIBBON. THIS WOULD BE APPROPRIATE FOR A BEDROOM DECORATED IN THE HIGH VICTORIAN STYLE.

Fig 8.3 Sewing the narrow lace to the deep lace.

about ⅞in (22mm) from the loop.

4 Snip the rod about 2in (51mm) from this bend.

5 Fit the end of the rod into the hole in the cradle.

6 Thread the ribbon through the length of one piece of deep lace. Neaten the ends by threading them back in at each end.

7 Gather the length of deep lace at the top with tiny running stitch, then tie the two thread ends together tightly so that the lace looks similar to a veil.

8 Sew this onto the loop of the brass

rod, and decorate with a ribbon bow tied through the loop.

9 Arrange the lace hood to hang over the brass rod and cradle.

Cradle trim

1 Measure the internal dimensions (long sides and base) of your cradle. Cut a piece of fabric for the lining, slightly larger than these measurements to allow for hemming. (My lining fabric measured 3⅛in (79mm) square once hemmed.)

2 Thread the ribbon through one of

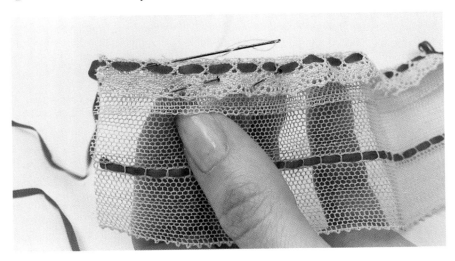

the narrow lengths of lace. Tie one end into a bow round one of the cradle knobs, and leave the free end long. Ease the resulting loop off the knob.

3 Fold over the top of a length of deep lace so that it is slightly shorter than the height of the cradle. Lay the narrow lace along the top of the deep lace and slip stitch the two together.

4 Slip the original loop back over the cradle knob, pull the ribbon in the narrow lace and gather it to the same length as the outside of one long side. Tie the ribbon into a tight bow round the opposite knob, and snip off to leave a long, free end.

5 Repeat steps 2–4 for the opposite side of the cradle.

6 Ease the bows off the knobs, lay the gathered-lace side trims along the edges of the lining fabric, and sew together.

7 Fit the lace-trimmed lining into the cradle by fixing the four loops back over the knobs. Trim the ribbon ends neatly.

8 Spray liberally with spray starch. Arrange the folds of the lace and the ribbon ends and leave to dry.

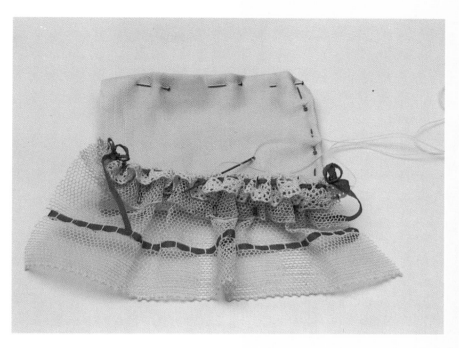

Fig 8.4 Sewing the side trim to the lining fabric.

Bedding

1 Cut a snippet of foam to fit the base of the cradle.

2 Cover this with a scrap of cotton fabric and press into the cradle.

3 Sew a tiny lace pillow and coverlet from scraps of old lace.

TECHNIQUE

Quick Quilting

Quilting enjoyed a revival amongst eighteenth and nineteenth century ladies, but dates back to the fifteenth century, originating in the monasteries and nunneries of the time.

Quilting is traditionally associated with bedspreads, but quilted cushions, laundry and knitting bags and even quilted chair covers look very attractive. Since I can only marvel at the skill of quilters who work in miniature, I hit upon this method when browsing through the fabrics in a sewing shop. It gives a convincing 'handmade' quilt effect without the painstaking needlework.

Keep a lookout for fabrics with a

small quilt print, and buy ¼yd (¼m) when you see it. I've found quite a variety on my travels. Prints incorporating squares and triangles work best: pentagons and octagons are far trickier to stitch using this 'quick quilting' sewing machine method. If you don't have a sewing machine, you can hand sew the quilt – but it will take longer. Simply replace the tacking stitch with fine backstitch.

A quilt doesn't have to be padded, but it does add to the authenticity. Very thin packing foam is ideal. (I have a collection of various pieces of packing foam, and have yet to buy a piece.)

KNOW-HOW
QUICK QUILTING

- If you use a simple square print, there's no need to work any tacking stitch before sewing.
- The more quilt lines you tack in, the more detailed the resulting quilt.
- You can customize the printed pattern by tacking in extra lines to make the quilted section smaller.
- If you can't find a fabric with a quilt print or want your quilt made up of a combination of particular fabrics, you can quilt a number of sections of plain or patterned fabrics and sew them together.
- Quick quilting 'shrinks' the size of the fabric by approximately half, so double the surface area required when cutting your fabric.
- It helps to roughly tack the seams in place before machining. Use a contrasting thread so that it's easy to spot and remove once the sewing is finished.
- Pull the tacking stitches out as you progress, before they become repeatedly sewn over and difficult to remove.
- If your fabric print is small, tack and sew as narrow a seam as you can or the pattern will disappear inside the seams. (The resulting quilt may also end up too bulky.)
- As the stitching progresses, the intersections get progressively harder to stitch through. Since this area is well and truly stitched, it does no harm to skip over it by lifting the foot of the sewing machine and moving the needle further on.
- Don't worry if some of the stitching puckers the quilt. When you have finished, carefully unpick the section with a sharp needle and restitch (by hand if necessary). Be very careful if you use a seam ripper!

Quilted Bedspread

QUILTED BEDSPREAD.

Pad only the central panel of the quilt and leave the sides empty. This helps it to drape over the bed more convincingly.

METHOD

Tacking

1. Measure the length and width of the bed. Cut the fabric twice this size.
2. Fold the fabric onto the right side and begin tacking along the top horizontal pattern line. Continue along each horizontal pattern line as you work down the fabric.
3. Working on the wrong side, tack a narrow seam along the line in contrasting thread. Working down the fabric, continue to tack all the horizontal lines of the pattern.
4. Turn the fabric 90° and tack along all the vertical pattern lines.
5. Continue with the bisecting lines, first left, then right, until all the pattern lines are tacked.

Materials

- Quilt print fabric
- Contrasting thread
- Matching thread
- Matching backing fabric
- Very thin packing foam

6. Tack extra quilt lines into the pattern if you want to refine the finished result.

Machine stitching

1. Select the smallest stitch length on your sewing machine. Systematically machine stitch along the tacking lines with matching thread, still working on the wrong side. Remove the tacking thread as you go. Continue until the

TIP

IF THE INTERSECTIONS BECOME HARD TO STITCH THROUGH, SKIP TO THE OTHER SIDE OF THE STITCHED AREA WITH THE MACHINE NEEDLE.

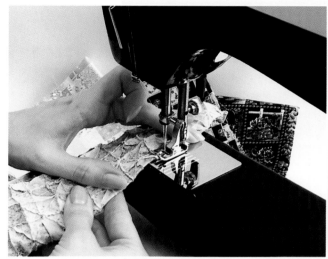

entire fabric is covered with machine stitching.

2 Check that the quilting is even and free of puckers on the right side of the fabric. If not, unpick the relevant area and restitch.

3 Press the quilt on the wrong side, with a cool iron.

Making up

1 Cut a section of backing fabric to fit the quilt. Stitch this to the wrong side of the quilting, along three sides only.

2 Lightly stitch a rectangle of thin packing foam, the size of the bed, in the centre of the wrong side of the quilt. Turn the quilt right side out.

3 Fold the raw edges of the fourth side under and slip stitch together neatly.

4 Press the quilt lightly on the back, with a cool iron.

ABOVE LEFT: *Fig 8.5 Tacking in the stitch lines.*

ABOVE: *Fig 8.6 Machine sewing the tacked stitch lines.*

VARIATIONS

TRY THIS ALTERNATIVE QUICK QUILTING METHOD. MACHINE STITCH TOGETHER STRIPS OF FABRIC $7/8$IN (22MM). CUT $7/8$IN (22MM) STRIPS FROM THE RESULTING PIECE. THIS WILL MAKE UNIFORM FABRIC STRIPS OF SQUARES. STITCH THESE STRIPS TOGETHER AGAIN IN A RANDOM PATTERN.

Fig 8.7 Sewing on the backing fabric.

KNOW-HOW
UPHOLSTERING

◆ Upholstery should feel soft to the touch, but don't over-stuff miniature furniture: it can soon take on a lumpy appearance.

◆ Choose a fabric that complements the period of the piece. Tapestry fabric is effective for the 1600s; stripes evoke the Regency era; a discreet regular pattern such as fleur-de-lis suits Georgian furniture; and traditional floral patterns suit the Victorian era. For Edwardian furniture, a William Morris-style fabric looks attractive.

◆ Favour natural fabrics such as silk, cotton or linen. These drape far better than synthetic fabrics.

◆ Full-size curtain fabric makes ideal miniature upholstery fabric. Search through the remnants box in curtain shops and collect likely specimens.

◆ Favour small patterns so that they look in scale.

◆ Symmetry is as important in miniatures as it is in full-size furniture. It's always best to match up the pattern. If the pattern is relatively large, you will need proportionately more fabric as there will be more waste when you centre and match the pattern. Place any large pattern centrally and match the joins where possible.

◆ The choice of trimming is as vital as the choice of fabric.

◆ If a complementary trimming cannot be found, it is often best to leave the furniture untrimmed until you find something suitable. Trimming which is out of scale, the wrong shade, or too modern can ruin the effect.

continued on page 89

TECHNIQUE
Fabric Upholstery

Since the wooden component of upholstered furniture isn't visible, it doesn't matter which type of wood you use. I generally use bits that come to hand. (An off-cut of wood sitting on my neighbour's front lawn came to hand as I was making the following Knole sofa.) You could even use balsa wood, which is the easiest wood of all to work with, but it doesn't give the reassuring weight we expect from quality furniture and it's not so sturdy.

Start saving packing foam. This is ideal under fabric or leather upholstery. It gives a smooth, even look to the finished piece, is springy to the touch and can be easily trimmed to size.

PROJECT
Knole Sofa

Knole sofas came into being around 1600, which makes them suitable for a seventeenth century setting onwards. Knole sofas have a rigid back, but the sides come down on ratchets, turning them into day beds. The sides are held up by cords tied round pegs. Model ship builders' belaying pins make ideal pegs. You can also adapt sections from banister spindles or even whittle your own from thin dowel. Instant tasselled cording can be gleaned from tasselled greetings cards or made from embroidery silk.

Materials

◆ 1in (25mm) wood blocks (for seat): 5½ x 2in (140 x 51mm)

◆ ⅛in (3mm) wood sheet (for arm pieces): 2in (51mm) square

◆ ⅛in (3mm) wood sheet (for back): 5½ x 3in (140 x 76mm)

◆ Thin packing foam

◆ Thick packing foam

◆ Tapestry fabric

◆ Matching thread

◆ Dark cotton fabric

◆ Matching cording

◆ Matching trimming

◆ Belaying pins x 4

◆ Wood glue

◆ Tacky glue

KNOLE SOFA.

METHOD

Making the frame

❶ Lay the seat piece so that the 2in (51mm) side is uppermost. Glue the wooden back piece, lengthways, to one of the 1in (25mm) sides with wood glue. Secure with an elastic band until dry.

❷ Drill a ¹⁄₁₆in (1mm) hole, ⅛in (3mm) from the end, on the sofa back and on one side of each arm piece. We'll fit pegs into these holes to hold the cord ties later.

❸ Glue a layer of thin foam to the sofa back, leaving a ⅛in (3mm) gap on each side for the arms to fit into.

❹ Fit a thicker piece of foam to the seat, leaving a ½in (13mm) gap either side for the upholstered arms, but don't glue yet.

❺ Glue a layer of thin foam to both wooden arm pieces, with a ¹⁄₁₆in (1mm) gap round the edge.

Covering the seat back

❶ If your fabric has a pattern, work out roughly where the pattern will lie before cutting it.

❷ Cut a length of fabric 7 x 12in (178 x 305mm). With the right side up and the raw edges folded under, lay the fabric over the seat back. Glue the back edge of the fabric under the seat block.

❸ Make any adjustments needed in the folded edges to completely cover both the front and back of the sofa back. Neatly slip stitch each side down as far as the seat block. Leave the rest of the fabric length unstitched for now. This will cover the seat and front.

Covering the arms

❶ Cut two lengths of fabric (with matching patterns), 4 x 6in (102 x 152mm), then cover both arm pieces, working one at a time, as follows.

❷ Working on the edge with the drill hole uppermost, lay the fabric right

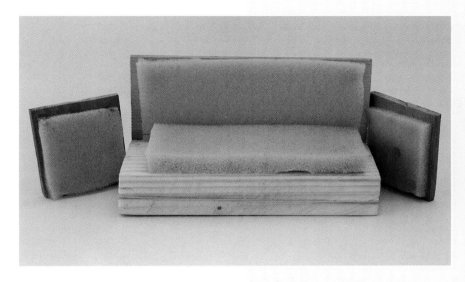

side up and raw edges folded under, over the wooden arm piece.

❸ Make any adjustment needed in the folded edges to completely cover the back and front of the arm piece. Neatly slip stitch each side together, but leave the end flaps, on the bottom, open.

❹ Locate the peg holes in the arms by probing with a pin. Position the arms so that their peg holes sit next to the peg holes at each end of the sofa back.

❺ On the padded side of the arm-piece only, trim the flap to a point. Smear tacky glue onto the wrong side of this flap, sit the arm on the seat block, and stick the flap to the top of the seat block. *Before* the glue dries, pull the arm down horizontally to ensure the fabric has enough leeway for the arm to lie flat. Repeat for the second arm.

❻ Smear the flap on the unpadded side of the armpiece very lightly with tacky glue and press onto the side of the seat block. Again, *before* the glue dries, make sure the fabric has enough leeway to allow the arm to be raised and lowered. Repeat for the second arm.

❼ Slip stitch together the resulting fabric joins at the back of the sofa, running from the arms down to the base of the seat.

Fig 8.8 Gluing the foam sections onto the wood pieces.

continued from page 88

◆ For an even finish, smooth the fabric into place before you sew.

◆ The right fabric tension is important in fabric upholstery. Pull the fabric tight to avoid dips and wrinkles, but not so tight as to cause puckering or straining at the seams.

◆ It's generally better to invest a little more time sewing the fabric joints together rather than using glue. Over time, thread is more durable than glue and your miniature will look better for longer.

◆ Reserve the use of glue for attaching fabric to the wood frame. When you *do* glue, use tacky glue and be very mean with it. Visible glue spots will spoil the finished effect.

◆ Latex glues are specialist fabric glues. They do a terrific job permanently gluing large areas of fabric, but they do discolour over time and aren't suitable for miniature work.

◆ Visible stitching can be disguised with decorative cording.

Fig 8.9 Covering the sofa back and sides with fabric.

TO MAKE A MORE MODERN
SOFA, MODIFY THE SHAPE OF
THE ARM RESTS AND FIX THEM
PERMANENTLY IN PLACE. TO
MAKE ROUNDED ARM RESTS,
GLUE ON SECTIONS OF DOWEL
BEFORE UPHOLSTERING (SEE
LEATHER WING ARMCHAIR,
PAGE 91).

The seat

1 Place the seat foam under the
unstitched fabric length left from
covering the sofa back. This length of
fabric was turned under at both sides:
tuck the foam inside these side folds so
that it isn't visible when the arms of the
sofa are down. Smear glue onto the
fabric side folds and press them onto
the seat block to secure the foam.

2 Pull the foam and fabric smoothly
over the seat block. Glue the fabric
overlap onto the base of the seat block.
Trim away any excess fabric. (I stitched
a tuck in my fabric at the back of the
seat to adjust the fabric pattern.)

3 Slip stitch together the resulting
fabric joins at the front of the seat
block, running from the arms down to
the base of the seat.

4 Glue a rectangle of dark fabric
over the fabric ends on the base of the
seat block, to neaten its appearance.

Cord ties

1 Apply a little tacky glue to the end
of the belaying pins and push them
through the fabric (no need to cut),
into the drill holes at the corners of the
sofa back and arms.

2 Tie cording to each pair of pegs, to
hold the pegs together, and fray the
ends of the cord to form tassels.

Trimming

1 Neatly stitch matching cording
along any visible joins to disguise the
stitching line.

2 Stitch matching trimming to the
base of the sofa.

Fig 8.10 Fitting belaying pins.

TECHNIQUE
Leather Upholstery

Upholstering with leather requires a slightly different technique from fabric. This is because it can't be stitched and must be glued in place. Raw edges spoil the finished effect, so the technique must leave no cut edges visible.

Discard all those old leather belts people give you to recycle into miniatures: thick leather is not suitable for miniature work. The thinner the leather, the easier it is to work with, so favour the very best quality, soft, pliable leather. Keep a lookout for bags of leather off-cuts as these can be suitable,

though if you're upholstering furniture, it's usually necessary to buy a square of thin, supple leather from a miniatures supplier. The professionals' secret to impressive leatherwork is polish. Leather polishes up so well it's practically a crime not to polish it.

Once you master the technique of working with leather you can cover any suitably shaped item. For example, try covering various small containers to make suitcases and trunks, and plastic dolls' shoes to make delightful miniature footwear.

PROJECT
Leather Wing Armchair

This chair is upholstered in brown leather and the woodwork is stained with Georgian Light Oak. I based it on a Georgian mahogany and green leather chair. You can use wood glue to assemble the structure, but epoxy resin is equally strong, and since it is quicker

LEATHER WING ARMCHAIR.

to dry it has the advantage of making the project progress more quickly.

Like the Knole sofa, this chair's structure is made from scrap wood. I used the wooden base of an old drawer. The pieces are shaped, so this project also demonstrates how to use a mini jigsaw to cut round curves. Mini jigsaws are not at all difficult to use. The technique is very similar to feeding fabric through a sewing machine and probably no more dangerous. Don't rush out to buy a mini jigsaw unless you plan to construct much of your own miniature furniture from scratch – you can also use a full-size jigsaw. Borrow one to see how you get on with it.

In the absence of any form of jigsaw, use a fret saw or coping saw fitted with a helical spiral fret saw blade. If you hunt around DIY shops you can also find lengths of spiral blades with gripping loops on the end. Helical or spiral blades allow you to saw in any direction.

KNOW-HOW
LEATHER UPHOLSTERING

◆ Glove leather is ideal for miniature work. Old leather gloves can sometimes be found at jumble sales and charity shops.
◆ Like fabric, leather must be pulled taut to look effective.
◆ For small accessories such as shoes, scrape as much of the backing from the leather as possible to make it thinner still.
◆ Use tacky glue to stick leather.
◆ Once your leather project is finished, rub in some standard clear shoe polish with a soft cloth. With a shoe buffer or scrap of fleecy fabric buff to a high shine – some elbow grease is also needed here.

JIGSAW

- Always keep a few spare jigsaw blades. It's very frustrating to snap your last blade in the middle of a project.
- Fit the jigsaw with a blade designed to cut wood.
- Keep the tiny key which tightens the chuck in a safe place, with the spare blades!
- Mark the cut line boldly in soft pencil.
- To ensure you cut accurately along the cut line, you will need to watch the blade closely as it saws. Always wear goggles to protect your eyes from splinters.
- Keep blowing away the sawdust so you can see the cut line clearly.
- Always keep the base plate flat against the wood surface. (This helps to avoid putting too much pressure on the blade, which may snap.)
- Be patient and gently guide the jigsaw through the wood without force. (If you must press, press downwards.) The blade is fragile; impatience will soon break it.
- Work on a sturdy, safe surface such as a workbench.
- Keep your fingers well away from the blade whether moving or not!

Fig 8.11 Cutting out the wooden patterns with a mini jigsaw.

METHOD

Seat structure

1 Trace four pattern pieces onto the wood sheet – the seat, the back and two side pieces – from Fig 8.12.

2 Carefully cut them out using a mini jigsaw or a helical blade fitted into a fret saw or coping saw.

3 Sand off the rough edges.

4 Glue the side pieces to the back piece with epoxy resin so that the side pieces will sit on top of the seat piece. Glue the seat piece beneath this assembly and support the structure until it is dry. (Gently prop the pieces together with wood block off-cuts or something similar. You can try an elastic band round the seat base, but be careful the pieces don't catapult away!)

5 Cut two lengths of dowel to measure 1in (25mm). Cut away a quarter of both dowel pieces with a junior hacksaw. The easiest way to do this is to place the dowel section in a mitre block. Saw halfway through the dowel, then turn a quarter turn and saw halfway through again until a quarter of the dowel comes away. Discard this section.

Materials

- ¹⁄₁₆in (1mm) scrap wood sheet
- Soft leather, 12in (305mm) square
- ⅜in (10mm) wooden dowel off-cut
- Wood strip, ¼in (6mm) square
- Epoxy resin
- Coarse sandpaper
- Thin packing foam
- Thick packing foam
- Clear shoe polish
- Tacky glue
- French polish
- Wood stain

6 Fit the dowel pieces over the chair arms and glue in place with epoxy resin (see Fig 8.13).

7 Once dry, round off the back end of the dowels with coarse sandpaper to blend in with the line of the seat.

Legs

1 Cut four lengths of square wood

TIP

AS ADHESIVE REPELS WOOD STAIN, YOU MIGHT LIKE TO STAIN THE WOOD STRIP BEFORE YOU BEGIN GLUING.

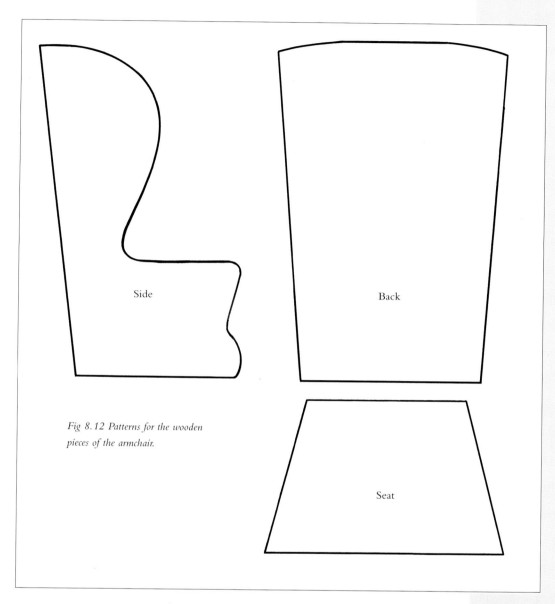

Fig 8.12 *Patterns for the wooden pieces of the armchair.*

Side

Back

Seat

strip to measure 1¼in (32mm).

2 Glue a leg to each corner of the chair base, with epoxy resin. *Before* the glue dries, square up the front leg with its corresponding back leg so that a stretcher (the strut between the front and back leg) can be glued in between. Carefully stand the chair up to check that it stands level, then leave undisturbed to dry.

3 To make the stretcher, mark off the length between one back and front leg and cut a length of wood strip to fit. Cut a similar stretcher for the other

pair of legs. Glue the stretchers in place with epoxy resin and leave to dry.

4 Measure and mark off the length between the two stretchers and cut a length of wood strip to fit between them. You will have to taper its end slightly as the back legs are closer than the front ones. Glue this final strut in place with epoxy resin.

5 If you haven't already done so, stain the legs and base of the chair, and set aside to dry.

6 Coat the legs with a couple of coats of french polish (see pages 62–5).

Upholstering the inner sides

1 Cut out two sides from the thin foam, using the pattern given in Fig 8.14. Glue them to the inner sides of the wooden frame, but leave a ⅛in (3mm) gap where the side joins the back and the base. (See Fig 8.15). The leather upholstery will be glued here.

2 Fold the excess foam over the edge, onto the outer side. Glue this down. Glue the foam over the front and side of the arm (the dowel section) of the wooden frame.

3 Using the pattern given in Fig 8.17, cut two pieces from the leather for the left- and right-hand sides. Apply glue to the wood left exposed around the foam padding on one side and stick the back and base edges of the appropriate leather piece here, overlapping onto

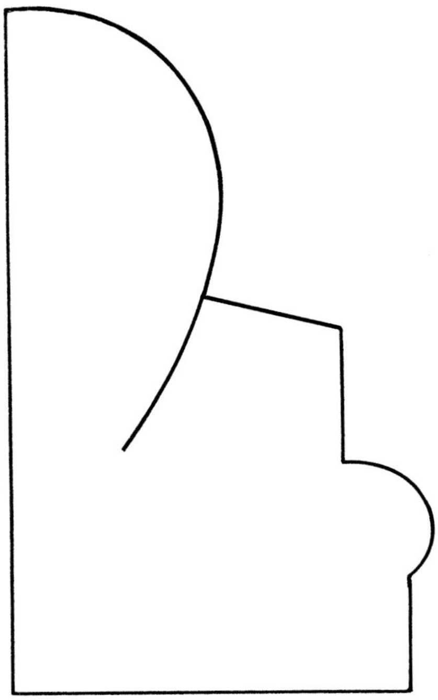

Fig 8.13 Assembling the wooden pieces to form the chair body.

Fig 8.14 Pattern for the foam piece for the side padding.

the wood seat and back pieces. *Before* the glue dries, adjust the position of the leather so that the corner of the arm lines up with the slit in the leather pattern.

4 Apply tacky glue around the curved edge of the outer side. Pull the leather slightly to tension it, then fold over the top curve of the frame and stick it down. Hold it in place so that it doesn't draw back as it dries. Systematically stick the rest of the overlapping edge to the outer side. You may need to ease the arm cover with a few snips to get a close fit. Pull the leather into place here as there won't be much slack.

5 Pull and stick the leather round the base edge (where the legs attach).

6 Pull and smooth the leather over the arm to minimize bumps.

7 Trim off any excess leather from the base and pare down any lumpy bits on the outside edge with a craft knife.

8 Repeat steps 4–8 for the second side.

FAR LEFT: *Fig 8.15 Gluing the foam pieces to both arms. (Also showing the leather folded over the side.)*

LEFT: *Fig 8.16 Gluing the leather pieces to both arms. (Also showing the foam folded over the side.)*

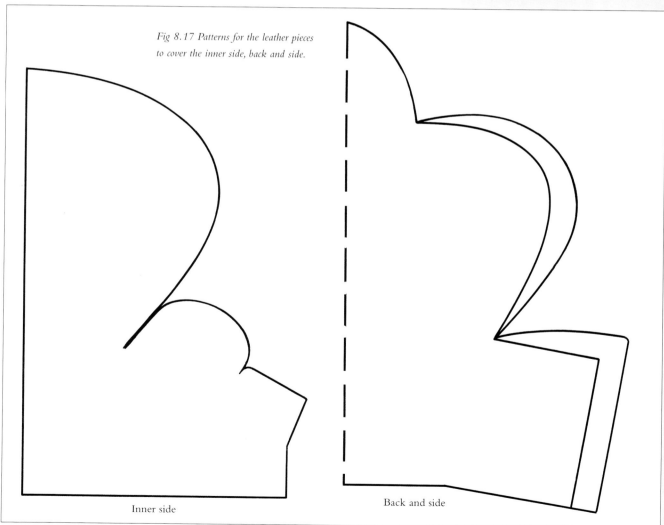

Fig 8.17 Patterns for the leather pieces to cover the inner side, back and side.

Inner side

Back and side

VARIATIONS

USING A MAHOGANY STAIN
AND GREEN OR RED LEATHER,
OR OTHER SUITABLE FABRIC,
WOULD BE EQUALLY
APPROPRIATE.

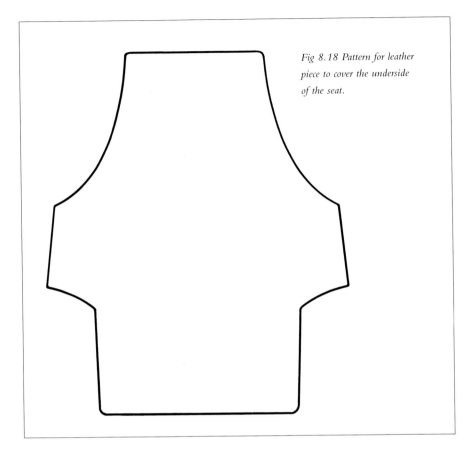

Fig 8.18 Pattern for leather piece to cover the underside of the seat.

Fig 8.19 Patterns for foam pieces for the back and seat padding.

Back

Seat

Upholstering the sides and back

1 Cut out one outer back and side piece from the leather, using the pattern given in Fig 8.17.

2 Apply tacky glue to the edge of the wrong side, fold and stick down on the pattern line to neaten the edge. Ease the corners with a few snips in order to achieve a neat finish.

3 Spread tacky glue thinly and evenly over the back and sides of the wooden framework. Press the leather outer piece onto the glue, smoothing and stretching it for a tight fit. (There should be enough 'give' in the leather to get it to fit, even if your wooden pieces vary slightly from the pattern.)

4 Pull the top flap over the top of the chair back and glue onto the inside.

5 Glue the overlap onto the base of the chair. Trim away the excess leather at each leg post.

6 Cut out the underside piece from leather, following the pattern in Fig

Fig 8.20 Gluing the back and seat pieces and covering the seat and back cushion.

8.18. Stick it to the underside of the chair, cutting space for the four leg posts. Pull the leather over the front seat edge and glue to the seat.

The back and seat

1 Cut out one piece for the back padding and one piece for the seat padding in thick foam, using the patterns given in Fig 8.19.

2 Cut out leather pieces to cover the back and seat padding pieces.

3 Cover the padding pieces with the leather by sticking the overlap onto the back of the foam with tacky glue.

4 Fit the back and then the seat piece into the armchair.

5 When completely dry, bring the leather to a high shine by applying clear shoe polish and buffing.

CHAPTER NINE

Modelling
Miniatures

Modelling Miniatures

*Successful modelling can't be rushed, but if you can devote time to perfecting the skill,
the results are among the most rewarding in miniaturism because your creation will be a unique
work of art. This chapter includes three of my favourite modelling media: polymer clay,
Milliput and papier-mâché, but the following tips can be applied to any medium.*

TECHNIQUE
Modelling with Milliput

Milliput is the best known brand of epoxy putty. It comes in standard yellow/grey, superfine white, silver/grey and terracotta. It combines the quality of modelling clay with that of glue and has three distinct uses:

◆ **As modelling clay** Superfine Milliput is the best choice for this. Once hardened it looks something like white china clay and can be drilled, sawn, sanded or painted. I prefer it to regular air-drying clay because it has a finer texture.

◆ **As permanent Plasticine** It can hold components together and will stick to most surfaces including metal, wood and plastic. This is useful if you need to stick a round-ended object, such as a bead, to a thin object, such as a cocktail stick. In this way, Milliput can be used as an alternative to solder.

◆ **To make moulds** Milliput can also be pressed into a mould and cast to make such things as tiny china dolls' heads.

Milliput comes in two sticks. To make the compound, blend equal amounts of each stick until the colour is uniform and free of streaks. If left at room temperature for two to three hours it will set rock hard. Smaller amounts harden more quickly. The hardening process can be speeded up with heat. (Leave the model on a warm radiator.)

PROJECT
Rococo Plaster Mirror

I used Milliput to decorate this wood-framed mirror, which was left over from a cheap imported dressing table which I made into a Georgian writing desk. Similar mirrors are often sold in dolls' house shops. Alternatively, you can frame a small mirror using the picture framing technique given in Chapter 12 (see page 139). Small mirrors can usually be picked up cheaply

KNOW-HOW
MODELLING

◆ Wash your hands before handling the medium, particularly if it is a pale shade. It will quickly appear grubby.

◆ Only model when you have sufficient time. (For me, this is when I'm cosily ensconced in front of the television.)

◆ When you have achieved a pleasing result, stop. Resist the temptation to overwork your model.

◆ Try to avoid leaving fingerprints on your model.

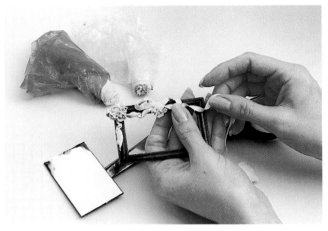

ABOVE: ROCOCO PLASTER MIRROR.

ABOVE RIGHT: *Fig 9.1 Modelling the Milliput decoration.*

KNOW-HOW
MILLIPUT

◆ Milliput can have a drying effect and act as an irritant on skin. Wear latex gloves for the blending stage and rinse your hands well after modelling.

◆ Soft Milliput can be difficult to model. Leave the blended Milliput to harden off for about 30 minutes before working with it. Don't forget about it though; it will harden to a solid lump in a few hours.

◆ Milliput can be rolled out like pastry to the required thickness. Use a section of brass tubing or even a smooth-sided ballpoint pen as a rolling pin.

◆ Once rolled out, Milliput can be cut into strips or shapes with scissors. It's easier to cut when it has hardened.

◆ Terracotta Milliput is useful for making garden troughs and flower pots.

in charity shops in the guise of hand-bag mirrors, budgie toys, or children's play mirrors.

METHOD

Preparation

1 Remove the mirror from its wooden frame and set it aside.

2 Blend a walnut-sized ball of Superfine Milliput. Set aside to harden for 15 minutes.

3 Roll the ball of Milliput into a long sausage and flatten to a thickness of about ½in (1mm). Cut this length into three strips about ³⁄₁₆in (5mm) long.

Materials

◆ Framed mirror
◆ Superfine Milliput
◆ Spray primer: white
◆ Acrylic paints: selection
◆ Gold marker pen
◆ Double-sided tape
◆ Clear spray lacquer

Bows

1 Make the central bow from one of the Milliput strips. You can't tie a bow in the regular way, so do this as follows. Stick the point about a quarter of the

Fig 9.2 Spraying with primer.

way down the strip to the centre of the strip to make a loop. This should leave a dangling end hanging from the centre.

2 Make an identical loop on the other half of the strip.

3 Wind one of the dangling ends tightly over the middle of the bow to form the knotted centre.

4 Carefully press the knotted centre of the bow to the top centre of the wooden frame.

5 Twist and drape the dangling ends to either side of the frame and press them into place. So far, the bow should only cover the top of the frame. If there is excess Milliput, pinch it off. (This doesn't have to be too neat as the ends will be covered with more bows.)

6 With the two remaining Milliput strips, make a bow for each corner in a similar way to the first bow, but smaller and with only one dangling end.

7 Press these bows onto each top corner, to cover the ends of the first bow.

8 Arrange the dangling ends of the small bows into twists and press them lightly onto the frame sides.

9 Trim the bow ends neatly and arrange the loops and folds of the Milliput bows attractively before setting aside to harden.

Roses

1 While the bows harden, make 12 rosebuds from Milliput. The technique, as follows, is similar to that used in sugar paste modelling. Pinch off a small piece of Milliput. Flatten it between your fingers so that it is very thin. Roll it up to make a tiny furled rosebud.

2 Pinch another tiny piece of Milliput and flatten it into a tiny petal shape. Decide which is the thinnest edge and stick the base of the petal to the rosebud base.

3 Repeat with two more petals.

4 When you have finished the rose,

roll the base between your fingers and thumb to make a short, thin stem. Pinch off all the excess Milliput; there might be quite a lot.

5 Make 12 rose leaves from Milliput as follows. Cut a leaf shape from flattened Milliput, with a craft knife. Mark on the veins with the back (the blunt side) of a craft knife.

6 Carefully press four buds and four leaves, in clusters, onto each bow (see Fig 9.2).

7 Set the decorated frame aside for a few hours until hardened.

Priming and painting

1 Spray the entire frame with a few thin coats of white primer. (This will help to disguise any fingerprints on the Milliput.)

2 Paint the mirror with acrylic paints. Two coats may be needed to get a good intensity of colour.

3 Outline the frame with gold marker pen. Set aside for 24 hours for the gold paint to dry completely.

4 Spray with a couple of coats of clear spray lacquer to give a glazed sheen.

5 Fit the mirror back into the frame and secure on the back with tape.

Fig 9.3 Painting and gilding the mirror.

FURTHER APPLICATIONS

TINY MILLIPUT DECORATIONS CAN BE APPLIED TO PLAIN LEAD ALLOY CASTINGS OR ORNAMENTS, THEN SPRAYED WHITE AND PAINTED TO GIVE THE EFFECT OF DECORATED CHINA SUCH AS MINTON.

Modelling with Polymer Clay

Polymer clay is a marvellous modelling medium. It is sold under various brand names such as Fimo (as in Fifi, the inventor's name), Formello and Sculpey. It comes in a wide range of colours and several different finishes. As modelling clays go, it is quite expensive, but well worth the money as it's so versatile, relatively easy to work with and needs no painting. Many different effects can be achieved; polymer clay lends itself particularly well to projects with swirls of colour such as marble. Every miniaturist should have a starter pack.

KNOW-HOW
POLYMER CLAY

◆ Be careful not to over-blend. The marble effect is soon lost and the resulting colour is drab and useless. This can be an expensive waste of clay.

◆ If the polymer clay becomes too soft to work, pop it into the fridge for a few moments to cool it off.

◆ 'Cook' or cure on a clean baking sheet.

◆ Transparent polymer clay is still quite fragile when warm, so allow the marble model to cool completely before you handle it.

◆ The marble effect can be enhanced with clear spray lacquer.

Marble Chess Table

'Marble' is the first thing beginners make with polymer clay. It's simply made by blending different colours. Polymer clay is also great for modelling objects such as chesspieces. (If the prospect of making 32 tiny chessmen daunts you, you can cheat by using a cast metal alloy set.)

The base of this marble chess table is a decorative egg stand (available from egg craft suppliers). The surround for the marble is a brass bangle: these can often be picked up in charity shops or jumble sales. The marble effect is made from black and transparent (more like waxy white) polymer clay. The checkered pattern is made using a paper template. Two table tops are cut and combined to make one checkered one, which is then hardened on ovenproof glass. As the clay warms and hardens it takes on a smooth marble-like finish from the glass surface. Be careful that the glassware doesn't get too hot and burn the clay.

Once the piece is finished, it's a good idea to fix the hardened chesspieces to the chessboard with Grip wax. This is a temporary sticking compound, available from dolls' house suppliers. It is preferable to Blu-tack because it's less noticeable and doesn't stain.

Materials

◆ Decorative egg stand
◆ Grip wax
◆ Brass bangle
◆ Grid paper, finely-squared
◆ Polymer clay: black, transparent and white
◆ Epoxy resin

METHOD

Making the templates

① On the finely-squared paper, mark out an 8 x 8 square grid of the size required for the chessboard (see Fig 9.5). The board's size will depend on the size of your egg stand and bangle.

MARBLE CHESS TABLE.

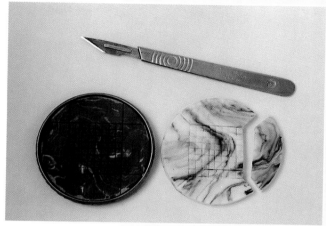

(My squares measured ⅙in (4mm) each.)

2 Place the bangle over the grid. Centre it by counting the squares. Draw round the inside of the bangle onto the paper (see Fig 9.5). Make two such identical templates.

3 Remove the bangle and draw a line down from each corner of the grid to the edge of the circle (see Fig 9.5).

Marble table top

1 Roll some thin strings of white polymer clay. Set these aside.

2 Soften half a block of black polymer clay. (This was enough to fill the bangle I used.) Knead the block briefly and shape into a square.

3 Lay the white strings across the black square and press them on. Stretch the square lengthways, widthways, backwards and forwards repeatedly until the white strings merge and blend. Briefly roll the clay into a ball and press flat again.

4 Shape the marbled black clay into a round slab.

5 Repeat the above process to make a round slab of marbled white clay using half a block of transparent polymer clay and black strings.

6 Roll out the two marbled slabs to cover an area slightly larger than the bangle. Ensure that the slabs are of a similar thickness.

7 Using the bangle as a pastry cutter, cut a circle from each slab. Smooth the top surface evenly with your finger.

8 Place the bangle over one of the slabs and place one of the prepared paper templates over the clay. Press it on lightly to help it stick.

9 Systematically cut through all the lines on the template, with a sharp craft knife. (See Fig 9.5.)

10 Repeat for the second slab.

11 Remove the bangle and place the slabs in the refrigerator for a few minutes. This will make the clay less likely to distort at the next stage.

12 Carefully remove one half of the board surround (two facing sides: see Fig 9.5) and discard (unless you want to make two table tops). Replace these sides with the corresponding pieces from the other slab so that a black edge sits next to a white edge.

13 Carefully remove alternate board squares and discard. Replace these with the corresponding pieces from the other slab to make the checkered pattern.

14 Place the bangle over this slab and gently stroke the resulting pattern to blend the edges together.

15 Place the clay slab, with the bangle surround, best face down on the ovenproof glassware. Gently press to ensure as much clay as possible is in

ABOVE LEFT: *Fig 9.4 Blending black and white 'marble' from Fimo.*

ABOVE: *Fig 9.5 Cutting the chessboard pattern in both blocks.*

contact with the glass. This will give it a smooth, stone-like finish.

16 Harden in a cool oven – 100°C (200°F) – for 10 minutes.

17 When the slab is cool, carefully lift it from the glassware.

18 Glue the slab to the egg stand with epoxy resin. (There is no need to spray the slab with clear lacquer as cooking on glassware produces the same effect.)

Pawns

1 Make the black pawns with the surplus black clay. If you have a Klay gun (a modelling tool for extruding clay or sugar paste), squeeze a thin line of black clay from it. If not, role a thin, even sausage about the thickness of a strand of spaghetti.

2 To make the base of the pawns, cut eight ⅟₁₆in (2mm) slices from the black strand. Place them flat-side down, on a clean baking sheet.

3 Cut eight more ⅟₁₆in (2mm) slices and roll each into an oval shape. Place these bodies gently on top of the eight flat bases.

4 To complete the black pawns, cut

four further slices in half and roll each half into a ball. Place a ball on each body.

5 Repeat the above process with the surplus white clay to make the eight white pawns, when you have completed the chesspieces and finished with the black clay.

Chesspieces

1 For the black chesspieces, roll eight ⅟₁₆in (2mm) slices into oval shapes, very slightly larger than the pawns' bodies, and place six of these onto eight flat bases.

2 Elongate two of the bodies and bend the top over slightly to make two knights. Pinch the top lightly and indent it with the back of a craft knife to make ears. Dot in eyes with a pin point if you like!

3 Roll two balls and place them on top of two bodies to make the bishops.

4 Cut five ⅟₂in (1mm) slices from the black sausage. Place two of these onto one body for the king. (The king is not finished yet.)

5 Press a castellated indentation onto the other three slices by pressing on three dents with the blunt side of the

BELOW: *Fig 9.6 The finished pattern with bangle replaced.*

BELOW RIGHT: *Fig 9.7 Mounting the table top on the egg stand.*

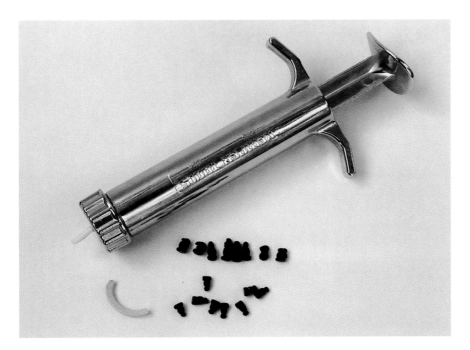

Fig 9.8 Modelling the chesspieces.

FURTHER APPLICATIONS

'MARBLED' POLYMER CLAY CAN BE USED TO MAKE A VARIETY OF MARBLE-EFFECT MINIATURES SUCH AS FIRE SURROUNDS, STATUES AND BATHROOM FITTINGS.

craft knife. Press the castle tops onto three separate bodies. Two of these make the rooks.

⑥ Place a tiny ball on top of the king (thus completed) and another on top of the third castle top to make the queen.

⑦ Harden all the pieces in a cool oven – 100°C (200°F) for 5–10 minutes.

⑧ Repeat with the leftover white clay to make the white chesspieces.

⑨ Secure the pawns and chesspieces to the board with Grip wax.

TECHNIQUE

Modelling with Papier-Mâché

Today papier-mâché is largely confined to the classroom, but during the nineteenth century it was a popular medium for making small furnishings and household articles. Originating in the Far East, papier-mâché reached Britain, via France, in the eighteenth century. It is a labour-intensive process using large sheets of paper impregnated with adhesive. A surprising variety of objects were made from papier-mâché, including sofas, tables, stools, cheval mirrors, cabinets, beds, pole screens, cradles, coal scuttles and even grand pianos.

Papier-mâché can be painted any colour, but since it was originally invented to resemble lacquerwork, the most

authentic colours are black, red and dark green. Finished models are sturdy, but light. An alternative to papier-mâché is bread dough which gives a similar effect.

You can buy ready-prepared packs of papier-mâché or mix your own. It's similar to making pastry. Either way it's a very cheap and versatile medium.

Papier-mâché recipe

① Finely shred about 20 sheets of kitchen roll.

② Mix this with a few tablespoons of children's water-based paste or gum.

③ Add a little boiling water and knead to a stiff, dough-like consistency with no dry spots.

KNOW-HOW

PAPIER-MÂCHÉ

◆ Papier-mâché takes several hours to harden so you can work at your leisure.

◆ Soggy papier-mâché is difficult to work with and takes days to dry.

◆ Have a cup of warm water handy to moisten your fingers.

◆ Like clay, papier-mâché can be modelled, pressed into, or wrapped round a master mould.

◆ Regular clay-modelling tools can be used to model papier-mâché, or just use your fingers.

◆ If carefully modelled and sanded, papier-mâché can imitate moulded plaster and carved wood.

◆ An embossed effect can be achieved with rubber stamps or the plastic stamps used in cake decorating.

◆ Unused papier-mâché can be stored in a sealed plastic bag in the fridge for about a week.

PROJECT
Papier-Mâché Chair

This type of papier-mâché chair would have been at the height of its popularity between 1835 and 1870. You can copy my interpretation, but better still, borrow some library books and work from original pictures.

This project is an example of the type of model that needs a wire framework. It doesn't matter how you make the framework; it need only be a very rough structure on which to apply the papier-mâché. The type, thickness and numbers of twists in the wire don't matter, and neither does neatness. The only consideration is how pliable the wire is: the more pliable the wire, the easier it will be to work with.

Once the model is thoroughly dry, it can be sanded smooth and spray painted. Either paint on your own decoration or decorate with transfers. (To make your own transfers, see Chapter 12, pages 136 and 137.)

METHOD

Twisting the framework

1 Begin at the centre of the wire. Don't worry too much about the measurements: if it looks right, it's fine. Bend the wire back on itself to make a 2in (51mm) front leg. Twist the leg loosely with pliers to hold it together.

> **TIP**
>
> TWIST THE WIRE AS OFTEN AS YOU LIKE – THIS WILL HELP TO ANCHOR IT.

2 Bend a 1¼in (32mm) length of wire round to make one seat side. At the end of this, twist a back leg measuring 1½in (38mm).

3 Bend the wire to form the back of the seat, 1½in (38mm) long.

Materials

- Pliable wire, 1yd (1m)
- Papier-mâché
- Primer: grey
- Spray paint: black gloss
- Acrylic paints: selection
- Thin gold marker pen
- Clear spray lacquer

PAPIER-MÂCHÉ CHAIR.

4 Working with the other end of the wire, bend a 1½in (38mm) length of wire to make the front of the seat.

5 Twist a second front leg, 2in (51mm) long.

6 Bend a second seat side, 1¼in (32mm) long.

7 Twist a second back leg, 1½in (38mm) long, to meet the other end of the wire. Twist the wire together here to complete the seat circle, incorporating the four chair legs.

8 Make the chair back by bending a new 7in (178mm) section of the wire. Twist this onto the main frame at one back leg and bend to meet the other back leg. Twist the free end of the wire

MAKING LARGE MODELS

- Large papier-mâché models, such as furnishings, need a wire framework.
- Pull off small pieces of papier-mâché from the ball and press onto the framework, building up the covering.
- Wet papier-mâché can be added to a dry model, so if you find modelling fiddly, work on one part of the model at a time, allowing this to dry before going on to the next part.
- When first applied, papier-mâché looks lumpy – it can easily be smoothed with your fingers to an even finish.

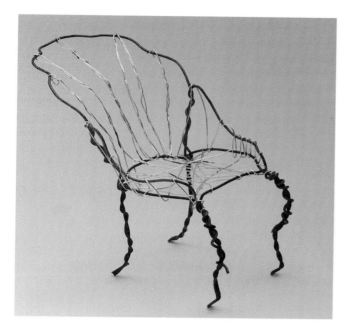

to the main frame at this point.

⑨ Twist one arm rest with this end of the wire and secure round the front leg. Snip off any excess.

⑩ Working with the remaining end of the wire, twist it up the opposite side of the back for 1in (25mm), and bend it to form the opposite arm rest. Twist the end of this round the other front leg. Snip off any excess wire.

⑪ Adjust the finished framework to make it look symmetrical.

Applying the papier-mâché

① This can either be done at one

sitting or one part at a time. Press small amounts of papier-mâché to all four legs, then squeeze it firmly on.

② Shape the front legs following the curve of the wire framework. Make the back legs fairly straight, with a small curve at the foot.

③ Shape the top of the front legs like a 'knee', then curve them in, out and in again at the foot (see Fig 9.10).

④ Shape the feet to give a graceful, tapering effect.

⑤ Press papier-mâché onto both sides of the seat.

⑥ Press papier-mâché onto both sides

ABOVE LEFT: *Fig 9.9 Twisting the wire frame.*

ABOVE: *Fig 9.10 Applying the papier-mâché.*

KNOW-HOW
DRYING

♦ Models can be worked for several hours before they dry solid, so you can leave your model for a while and return to it to refine the shape.

♦ To make a faster setting modelling compound, dissolve a few teaspoons of plaster or Polyfilla in the water.

♦ Your finished model will need at least 24 hours to dry out fully. It will pale in colour and become lighter.

♦ Drying can be speeded up by using a hair dryer or placing the model on a heater or in a cooling oven.

♦ Don't paint the model until it is completely dry. Once dry, papier-mâché can be sanded, sawn and drilled.

FAR LEFT: *Fig 9.11 Priming the chair.*

LEFT: *Fig 9.12 Spraying the chair black.*

Fig 9.13 Decorating the chair with acrylic and gold paint.

FURTHER APPLICATIONS

SMALL ARTICLES, SUCH AS PICTURE FRAMES, TRAYS, BLOTTERS, LETTER RACKS AND INK STANDS, CAN BE CAST FROM A MASTER MOULD CARVED FROM BALSA WOOD. PRESS PAPIER-MÂCHÉ INTO THE MASTER MOULD, HAVING FIRST COATED THE MOULD WITH WASHING-UP LIQUID TO PREVENT THE PAPIER-MÂCHÉ FROM STICKING. MANY COPIES CAN BE MADE IN THIS WAY. CONTAINERS SUCH AS TEA CADDIES, BOXES AND COAL SCUTTLES CAN BE MADE BY WRAPPING GLUE-SOAKED STRIPS OF PAPER OVER A WOODEN BLOCK.

of the back and arms.

7 Spend some time shaping the papier-mâché. When you are happy with the shape, finish by smoothing the surface. Set the model aside to dry for 24 hours.

8 When thoroughly dry, sand away any lumps with fine grade sandpaper.

Painting

1 Spray with several thin coats of grey primer until the surface is relatively smooth. Sand between coats if need be.

2 Spray with two or three coats of black gloss spray paint.

3 Paint a simple floral pattern onto the chair back.

4 Add a little gilding to the outline with a gold marker pen.

5 Finish by spraying with a coat or two of clear spray lacquer.

Customizing Furniture

Customizing Furniture

How can the amateur get instant results with practically no work? By customizing cheap imported furniture. Boxes and carded packs of wooden furniture (of varying quality), sold more as novelties than collectors' pieces, can often be picked up in seaside gift shops and on market stalls. The individual pieces are a pound or two and the sets are usually less than ten pounds. These sets are sometimes scorned by the miniaturist purists. And rightly so if you leave them as they are, but since all the woodworking has already been done, the fun of customizing can start immediately. A commonplace piece can soon be transformed into something unique. The following projects are a few ideas of mine. Once you get hooked on customizing cheap furniture, you're sure to come up with some great ideas of your own.

KNOW-HOW
SPRAY PAINTING

- Always spray paint in a well-ventilated area, preferably outside. If you suspect that you are sensitive to paint fumes, invest in a face mask.
- Spray paint is excellent for speeding up a painted project and giving a smooth, professional finish.
- Several thin coats will give a better finish than one heavy coat, which may run.
- To get an even finish, don't squirt a jet of paint at the piece, spray backwards and forwards across the furniture, keeping the can moving all the time. It's sometimes easier to move the object by turning it round on a piece of newspaper.

TECHNIQUE
Spray Painting

Small cans of acrylic spray paint are available from craft and model shops. These are fine for a small project, but cellulose car spray paints (available from auto shops) are far more economical for larger projects. The grey and white primers are worth investing in since most painted projects benefit from priming. The clear spray lacquer is also economical and suitable for most projects.

PROJECT
Georgian Clothes Press

I transformed this roughly finished, shelved cupboard into a Georgian clothes press. Since clothes hangers weren't invented until the turn of the twentieth century, pre-Edwardian wardrobes consisted of shelves rather than hanging rails. Clothes were sometimes hung on pegs inside the wardrobe, which was also called a 'linen press' or 'clothes press'.

I decorated the exterior with turned wooden beading (available from specialist dolls' house suppliers). I also glued on cheap metal filigrees. On the top half of the cupboard I glued two metal filigree decorations which resembled frames. Behind these I fitted small, cameo-style catalogue clippings. Eighteenth-century ladies, children or Madonnas would also be suitable. I coated the pictures with a few coats of transfer emulsion to finish them.

I also replaced the original handles to have them more in keeping with the period. Drawer pulls can be made from the eyes of hook and eye fastenings. Ideally, use old brass ones, which can often be found at the bottom of charity shop button boxes. Cupboard pulls can easily be made from small beads and filigrees, such as bell caps, drop beads and jump rings. If they look a little bright, distress them with a proprietary patinating fluid or simply use a dilute brown acrylic wash.

METHOD

Preparation

1 Sand the wardrobe lightly to remove any lumps or bumps. Remove the drawers. Remove the handles and drawer pulls.

2 Cut the decorative beading to size with a junior hacksaw and glue it to the wardrobe with tacky glue. Secure the beading with elastic bands until the glue dries.

3 Glue the decorative metal filigrees in place with superglue.

4 Blu-tack the metal filigree frames to the wardrobe doors, one on each side. This is a temporary attachment because later we will place pictures behind the frames. Ensure that the Blu-tack doesn't show as it will prevent the spray paint covering the area completely.

Painting

1 Spray the cupboard and drawer with several thin coats of white primer. Allow to dry, and sand lightly between coats to give a smooth finish.

2 Spray the cupboard and drawer with several thin coats of off-white spray paint.

Pictures

1 Remove the frames from the

GEORGIAN CLOTHES PRESS.

Materials

- Cheap wooden wardrobe
- Decorative beading
- Decorative metal filigrees
- Frame-like filigrees
- Spray primer: white
- Spray paint: off-white, e.g. Volkswagen Pastel White
- Cameo-style picture clippings x 2
- Transfer emulsion
- Fine gold marker pen
- Large brass eye fastening, from hook and eye
- Tiny brass nails x 2
- Blu-tack
- Small fluted bell cap
- Superglue
- Gold drop bead
- Tacky glue
- Gold seed bead
- Sandpaper
- Thin brass fuse wire

cupboard doors. The primer and paint may have stuck them fast, so you may need to gently pry them off with a blunt knife.

2 Remove and discard all the Blu-tack.

3 Paint over the pictures with a

CUSTOMIZING FURNITURE

- When buying cheap furniture sets, look primarily at the construction. It doesn't matter if the overall finish is poor or even if a bit has come unglued, but unless you want a skewed effect to represent aged or rustic furniture, choose pieces that are squarely glued together. You can sometimes re-glue sections, but don't bank on it.

- Be bold. Sometimes the more outlandish the idea, the better the end result. This furniture is so cheap, you can afford to experiment.

- Have a specific style in mind before you begin work. Look through antique books for inspiration.

- Replace trimmings such as handles with more authentic-looking fittings. For example, replace the gold string on a wooden harp sold as a Christmas tree ornament, with the finest brass beading wire. This will greatly improve its appearance.

- Add your own authentic touches. For example, the plastic netting sometimes found over vegetable boxes makes convincing brass grill when sprayed gold. Such grill was often used on Georgian cabinets.

Fig 10.1 Gluing filigrees and decorative beading to the cupboard.

SPRAY PAINTING OFF-WHITE AND GILDING IS A QUICK AND EASY WAY TO GIVE CHEAP FURNITURE AN AUTHENTIC GEORGIAN LOOK. TRANSFORM A BEDROOM 'SET' AND FURNISH A WHOLE ROOM WITH A GEORGIAN LOOK.

couple of coats of transfer emulsion to protect and finish them. Allow each coat to dry.

4 Glue the frames over the cameo-style clippings, centring the pictures.

5 Glue the framed pictures back in place permanently with tacky glue (see Fig 10.4).

Door handles

1 Thread the gold seed bead onto a length of thin brass fuse wire. Bend the wire up at the base and double it back over the bead.

2 Thread the gold drop bead, followed by the fluted bell cap, onto the brass wires.

3 Thread the brass wires into the old handle's hole on the cupboard door.

4 Glue the bell cap over the hole.

5 Bend and secure the wire to the back of the cupboard door, with glue.

Drawer pull

1 Pull the eye fastening apart slightly with pliers.

2 Bend the thread holes forward slightly.

RIGHT: *Fig 10.2 Priming the cupboard.*

FAR RIGHT: *Fig 10.3 Painting the cupboard off-white.*

Fig 10.4 Fitting the handles and picture inserts.

3 Grip the centre of the eye with pliers and straighten the curve.

4 Place the drawer pull in place on the drawer front, mark the thread holes and drill two tiny holes.

5 Glue the eye onto the drawer, positioning the thread holes over the drill holes.

6 Push a tiny brass nail into each thread hole to secure the drawer pull.

Gilding

1 Lightly trace over the raised filigree with the fine gold marker pen to highlight it.

TECHNIQUE
Lacquering

Lacquered furniture dates back to the seventeenth century. It is very easy and fun to reproduce. Lacquering furniture in the Oriental style is called japanning. The most common colours for japanned furniture are black, red and green, decorated with designs in gold. Dark green lacquered furniture has European origins. The finish on full-size lacquered furniture was achieved by applying layer after layer of varnish hardened by heat. We can achieve a similar effect in miniature by applying several thin coats of car spray paint on a cheap piece of furniture.

PROJECT
Japanned Bureau

Usually I japan in black, but I was really pleased with this red bureau. Renault Red 705 (cellulose car spray paint) is a good shade for red lacquer. Don't forget to pay attention to the innards too. I also added a small brass lock plate to the front, which sets the piece off nicely.

KNOW-HOW
LACQUERING

♦ Don't try to hand paint a lacquered finish. Brush strokes will not give the smooth sheen required.

♦ There are several types of black spray paint, from gloss to matt. I find that satin works best for a lacquered effect.

♦ Don't be daunted decorating your lacquerwork. It's just a case of scribbling on some eastern-looking doodles with a fine gold marker pen. In fact, the more you ponder and worry; the more daunting it will get. Study some decorated oriental furniture, practise on a piece of scrap paper, then go for it!

♦ Begin by outlining in gold. You can use a rule on the flat surfaces to help make the lines straight. (Be careful not to smudge the line as you remove the rule.)

♦ If, like me, you're no artist, it's best to stick to naturalistic designs such as birds, flowers, hills, rivers, trees and grasses. There's a larger margin for error here.

♦ If you don't like the effect, act quickly. Wipe off the design with a piece of kitchen paper. If the worst comes to the worst, leave to dry then spray over and start again.

♦ Be sure to allow gold marker pen 24 hours to dry.

ABOVE RIGHT: *Fig 10.5 Sanding the original bureau.*

ABOVE: JAPANNED BUREAU

METHOD

Painting

1 Lightly sand the bureau to remove any bumps. Remove all the handles and knobs. Gently prize off the hinge and remove the drawers.

2 Prime the bureau and drawers with half a dozen thin coats of grey primer. Lightly sand again once dry.

3 Spray with another half dozen thin coats of red spray paint. Allow each coat to dry for 10 to 15 minutes

Materials

- ◆ Cheap bureau
- ◆ Spray primer: grey
- ◆ Spray paint: Renault Red 705
- ◆ Fine gold marker pen
- ◆ Clear spray lacquer
- ◆ Brass lock plate
- ◆ Snippet of green leather
- ◆ Sandpaper

between coats. Build up a smooth, shiny coating of paint. Allow the coats of paint to harden overnight.

4 Replace the hinge.

Decoration

1 Trace round the outlines of the bureau and drawers with a fine gold marker pen. Apply as much or as little decoration as you like. Gold marker pens are solvent-based – leave to dry for 24 hours. This will prevent the outline smudging as you draw on the design.

2 Draw on some Oriental designs. It's a good idea to begin on the sides and finish on the front as you will probably improve as you work. Leave to dry for 24 hours.

3 Coat the bureau and the front of

Fig 10.6 Priming the bureau in grey.

FURTHER APPLICATIONS

SMALL ITEMS SUCH AS CHESTS AND BOXES CAN ALSO BE JAPANNED IN THIS WAY. OTHER FURNITURE SUITABLE FOR JAPANNING INCLUDES CABINETS, BUREAUX, COFFEE TABLES, CHAIRS, PIANOS, LONG-CASE CLOCKS, AND EVEN FOUR-POSTER BEDS.

the drawers with a couple of coats of clear spray lacquer.

Finishing

1 Glue the handles and drawer knobs back in place.

2 Stick a small rectangle of thin green leather to the inside of the bureau flap.

3 Add a small brass lock plate to the front if desired.

Fig 10.8 Applying the gold decoration with marker pen.

- Gilding is best achieved by spray painting.
- Gold spray paint can often be picked up cheaply after Christmas.
- Cellulose car spray paint comes in several shades of gold.
- Different shades of gold give different effects. Ford Arizona Gold gives an attractive antique gold effect and Vauxhall White Gold is ideal for gilded furniture.

TECHNIQUE
Gilding

Gilding means covering in gold. Gilt furniture has been popular throughout the centuries, and particularly during the eighteenth century. Unless your dolls' house is palatial, it is generally best to be sparing with gilt furniture: a few tastefully gilded pieces will have more impact than a roomful.

GILTWOOD THREE-PIECE SALON SUITE.

PROJECT
Giltwood Three-Piece Salon Suite

Not all furniture suits a gilded finish. Giltwood furniture tends to be of a classical eighteenth- and sometimes nineteenth-century design. A pair of eighteenth century carver chairs (with arms for the person who carves) work well. The Victorian balloon back style of chair also lends itself to gilding. I decided to give a cheap imported furniture set a Louis XVI face-lift.

I was pondering on how to simulate the carved edging to the suite when an '18 carat gold-tone' curb chain dropped through the letterbox; a gift from some grateful mail-order company from whom I have never ordered. On it went. Thickly twisted picture frame wire can be used to equally good effect as it also resembles ornately carved wood. I also glued a gilt filigree to the centre of the sofa for added decoration. Careful choice of fabric is vital to complete the finished effect. For further authenticity, I added some padding to the seat arms.

Materials

- Cheap three-piece suite
- Chain
- Decorative filigree
- Spray paint: gold
- Clear spray lacquer
- Thin card
- Tacky glue
- Thin foam
- Sandpaper
- Suitable fabric

Fig 10.9 The original suite.

METHOD

Preparation

1. Carefully remove the upholstery, but save it to make templates from later. (Lever it off with a blunt dinner knife.)
2. Lightly sand the furniture to remove any unsightly lumps and bumps.
3. Glue the chain round the sofa and chair backs with superglue.

Painting

1. Spray with three or four thin coats of gold spray paint, allowing the paint to dry between coats.
2. Finish with a coat or two of clear lacquer to give a sheen and protect the paint finish.

Upholstering

1. Cut new card bases out of thin card for the various seats and backs. Use the old upholstery pieces as templates.
2. Glue pieces of thin foam to the bases, trimming to size.
3. Cover the pieces with fabric, gluing the overlap onto the back of the card.

> **TIP**
>
> CAREFULLY MATCH AND CENTRE THE FABRIC PATTERN FOR BEST EFFECT.

4. Glue the upholstery pieces into place on the suite.

> **TIP**
>
> TRY TO KEEP GLUE AWAY FROM THE FABRIC WHICH IS TO BE VISIBLE. OVER TIME, SOME GLUES WILL DISCOLOUR FABRIC.

Fig 10.10 Removing the upholstery and gluing on the chain decoration.

Arms

① Cut a length of fabric 1in (25mm) longer than the arms. Fold a small 'hem' at both ends onto the wrong side. Roll the other sides to meet in the middle and pin to make a sausage shape.

② Stitch along the join, catching the 'hems' in at the top and bottom.

③ Carefully glue the sausage shape to the arm of the chair, stitch-side down.

Fig 10.11 Spraying the suite gold.

VARIATIONS

THIS GEORGIAN-STYLE SUITE WOULD LOOK EQUALLY EFFECTIVE SPRAYED WHITE AND GILDED.

Fig 10.12 Making the replacement upholstery.

Miniature Crafts

Miniature Crafts

Many miniaturists enjoy full-size crafts. Have you thought about adapting your favourite craft to miniature work? Mass production means crafts can easily die out. Learning or honing a skill can hold much satisfaction. You can even commission a talented friend or relative. What better birthday or Christmas present? Explain that their work will gain pride of place in your dolls' house and be preserved for future generations to admire. Make up a tiny book containing information about who made what and when and keep this book in the dolls' house. A watercolour, a knitted bed-spread and a cross stitch picture are a few of my recent commissions. I also have crocheted dollies, a tatted tablecloth, a Meo appliqué carpet, a lace runner and a pulled threadwork tablecloth.

Assure your crafters that they may take as long as they need, and supply all the miniature materials. Knitters, for example, will need the appropriate size knitting needles and single ply wool (knitting machine wool works well). Supply simple full-size patterns or a specialist miniature knitting pattern. Specialist miniature haberdashery suppliers will advise on what's needed for miniature crafts. (Find their details in dolls' house magazines, available on the newsstand.)

As well as knitting patterns, there are also 1/12 scale crochet and tatting patterns. Other crafts, such as macramé and lace, can be adapted from doily and bookmark patterns. When working in miniature, it's best to keep the pattern as simple as possible.

With luck, word will get round and your relatives and friends will be vying to get in on the act. Not everyone is able to work in miniature. Success often depends on good eyesight, but manual dexterity also plays its part. Explain this beforehand to avoid crestfallen relatives.

The following projects are just a few examples of crafts you can have a go at right now, without any previous skill. Practise the technique before embarking on the project: if your technique improves halfway through the project, you may be disappointed with the result.

Fig 11.1 Miniature work commissioned from friends and relatives.

TECHNIQUE
Hooked Work

Hooked work is the ancient craft of making mats for the kitchen or farmhouse. It's simply a process of pulling wool through canvas. Any loose-weave cotton, such as calico, is suitable for the canvas backing. It doesn't matter which type of wool you use; I picked up a bundle of discontinued tapestry wool colours in a craft shop. You can some-times find such bundles in charity shops. A rug hook is used for full-sized work, but a crochet hook is ideal for miniature hooked work. Use a hook that fits comfortably through the holes in your canvas and is large enough to pick up one strand of wool. You're sure to be able to pick up a suitable crochet hook in a charity shop.

HOOKED MAT.

PROJECT
Hooked Mat

Any simple design can be used to make this welcoming doormat. Text such as 'Welcome' or the name of the household could be used, but a simple picture is easiest for the beginner.

METHOD

Preparation

① Draw the outline of the required mat on the calico with a soft pencil. My door-mat measures 2¼ x 1⅝in (57 x 42mm).

Materials

- ◆ Wool: various colours
- ◆ Scrap of calico
- ◆ Soft pencil
- ◆ Embroidery tambour or large bangle and rubber band
- ◆ Tacky glue

② Draw a simple design onto the calico mat. I drew a very simple house.
③ Fix the calico over a large bangle, centring the pattern, and secure with

Fig 11.2 Hooking the outline and motif.

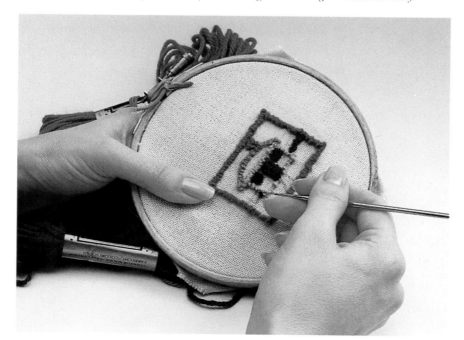

KNOW-HOW
HOOKED WORK

- ◆ As you fit the fabric into the frame, be sure to keep the weft and warp threads straight. This makes it easier to hook through the holes of the fabric, and the resulting pattern will be straight.
- ◆ It doesn't matter how you hold the hook and wool. As you work you'll settle into the most comfortable way.
- ◆ Use a single strand of any wool which can be picked up by your chosen hook. (Separate the strands in plied wool.)
- ◆ Keep the canvas taut as you work. It's a good idea to fit the canvas into an embroidery tambour (frame) if you have one. You can improvise one by placing a thick rubber band round a large metal, plastic or wooden ring, such as a large bangle.
- ◆ Don't worry too much about how the back looks.

Fig 11.3 Filling in the motif.

A HOOKED RAG RUG CAN BE MADE IN A SIMILAR WAY. HOOK VERY THIN STRIPS OF FABRIC THROUGH A LARGE WEAVE FABRIC SUCH AS SACKING. FOR MINIATURE WORK, VERY THIN STRIPS — AS THIN AS YOU CAN MAKE — OF ACRYLIC FABRIC WORK BEST AS THEY HOLD TOGETHER BETTER AND DON'T FRAY.

a rubber band. (Alternatively, fit the calico into an embroidery tambour.)

4 Ensure that the fabric is taut and that the weft and warp are straight.

Working the design

1 Begin by hooking the outline of the mat. Hold the strand of wool beneath the calico, push the crochet hook into a hole in the calico, catch the wool strand with the crochet hook and pull it through the same hole. Adjust the size of the resulting loop to

make it as small as possible.

2 Push the hook through the next hole and catch a second loop of wool. Pull this through the second hole and match the size of the loop to the first one. Continue in this way until the outline is complete.

3 Hook the outline in the main motif in the same way.

4 Fill in the spaces round the outlines, working horizontally along the threads.

Making up

1 When the entire pattern is worked, cut the mat from the frame, leaving a border of unworked calico.

2 Fold the excess calico onto the back of the mat and stitch or glue in place.

Fig 11.4 The completed pattern.

TECHNIQUE
Basketry

Basketware looks attractive in any period of dolls' house. There's plenty of scope to basketry if you take to it. Small baskets can hold bread rolls, fruit or vegetables. You can weave wastepaper baskets, shopping baskets, workbaskets, cribs, trays, pet baskets, picnic hampers, chairs and even lampshades.

You will need the thinnest of cane available. I have recycled thin cane from cheap wicker tablemats by soaking the mat and carefully unravelling it. Size 00 and 000 cane is available from specialist suppliers; ask in your local dolls' house shop. Cane is very cheap so you can afford to experiment.

Basket weaving technique

The base

1. Cut six stakes about 7in (178mm) long.
2. Hold three stakes over the other three to make a cross. You'll need to hold the stakes in place until they are secured by the weaver.

Pairing

1. Loop a length of dampened cane over one set of three stakes. Make the bend for the loop a little off-centre, so that the weavers don't run out at the same time.
2. Take the left-hand weaver in front of the stakes, over the top of the right-hand weaver, and round the back of the next set of stakes. Make sure the weaver comes back to the front. (See Fig 11.5.)
3. Repeat round the next set of stakes and continue pairing round the remaining two sets of stakes until you are back where you started. Once round all the stakes is one **round**. That's all there is to it!
4. Pair a further round. This will secure the central stakes in place – you can let them go now.
5. Soak the base and ease the stakes out to be evenly spaced. Continue pairing round the base in the same way, but this time pair round each separate stake, rather than round groups of three.

The upsett

1. When the base is large enough you will need to change direction so that the weave goes up. This is called the **upsett**.
2. Soak the basket then gently bend the stakes to a 90° angle.
3. Carry on pairing. If you want your basket to taper out, gradually weave more loosely, shaping the basket as you work.

Starting a new weaver

1. Wait until the weaver to be renewed is 'inside the basket', bend it back and slip in a new weaver beside it, on its right. Carry on weaving – the old end will sit inside the basket.
2. Trim it tidily when the basket is finished.

Border

1. Once the basket has reached the required height, snip the stakes back to leave about 2in (51mm).
2. Soak the basket to soften the stakes.
3. Taking one of the stakes, bend it down to take it behind the next stake, then in front of the following one, and behind the next. Leave the remaining length of the stake pointing inside the basket.
4. Repeat with the next stake and continue all the way round the basket top until all but the last stake is secured beneath the next.
5. Thread this last stake into the empty loop made by the first one.
6. Trim off the stake ends inside the basket with sharp manicure scissors. Trim close, but not so close that the stakes slip out from beneath their neighbour.

Handles

1. Soak two 2in (51mm) lengths of cane. Thread these into one of the stake holes along with the stake. Use a cocktail stick to help the cane down.
2. Twist the canes together a couple of times, then carefully bend them over to form a handle.
3. Thread the ends into the next stake hole.
4. Fit a second handle opposite the first.
5. Adjust the handles to make them evenly sized by pushing them further into the basket.

KNOW-HOW

BASKETRY

◆ Keep the coil of cane tidy or you'll spend more time untangling your cane than weaving your basket. Just before you begin work, remove the sticky tape from the coil and replace it immediately with a large rubber band.

◆ Miniature basketry is best kept as simple as possible.

◆ Size 00 and 000 cane is delicate so try to avoid kinking it. Store it carefully in a plastic bag.

◆ Remember to keep the cane moist. Fine cane dries out quicker than regular cane, so keep a bowl of warm water to hand to dip your work in. You can also moisten it with a damp sponge.

◆ When you finish weaving, stop at a full round so that each stake is woven to the same height.

◆ Tight work is important in miniature weaving, particularly when weaving the base, which shouldn't be too gappy. Pull down on the weaver as you work. Keeping the weaver damp also helps to pull it tighter.

◆ As you pair, ensure that the left-hand weaver always passes over the top of the right-hand one as it goes behind the stake. If you switch directions mid-weave, it will interrupt the line of the weave.

◆ If your weaver keeps snapping or fracturing – this looks like lots of little elbows in your work – your cane has dried out.

◆ If your stakes kink as you work this may be because the stakes are the same size as the weaver. They should be one size thicker.

◆ Cane can be dyed with tea, coffee or wood dye. It can also be spray-painted.

The central ribs of a basket are known as the **stakes**. The length that is woven round is called the **weaver**. The stakes should be one size thicker than the weaver. The best method of weaving for miniature work

PROJECT

Linen Basket

A linen basket is simple, but looks impressive. Once you have made the base and worked the upsett, the rest is simply a case of weaving to the required height. The lid is made in the same way as the base. (See Basket Weaving Technique, page 123.)

Materials

◆ 00 cane
◆ 000 cane

METHOD

Base

❶ Cut six lengths of 00 cane to measure 9in (229mm). These are the **stakes**.

is **pairing**. Before weaving, soak the weaver for a few minutes in warm water to soften it. Once you are familiar with weaving technique, you will find your work progresses very quickly.

LINEN BASKET.

❷ Lay three stakes over the other three to make a cross. Hold the cross in place while you pair round the four sets of stakes for two rounds, with a length of 000 weaver cane. (Use a length which is just short of being cumbersome and knotting up: about 2yd (2m) is good if you can manage it.)

Fig 11.5 Pairing the first round.

Fig 11.6 Pairing round the base.

3 Soak the cane and gently separate the stakes so that the twelve stakes are evenly spaced. Pair for seven rounds or until the base measures 1½in (38mm).

4 Soak the base, and **upsett** by bending the stakes to 90°.

5 Pair up for 19 rounds or until the basket reaches 1⅜in (35mm) in height.

As you weave, gradually flare the basket outwards.

6 Soak the basket, snip the stake-ends down to 2in (51mm) and work the border.

Handles

1 Soak two 2in (51mm) lengths of

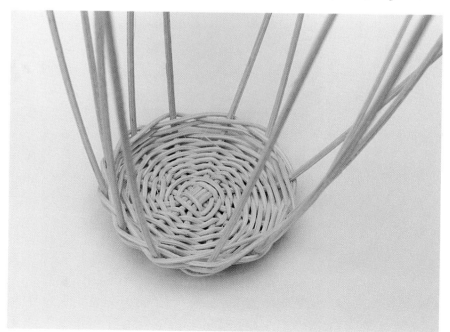

Fig 11.7 Weaving the upsett.

VARIATIONS

FOR A DIFFERENT EFFECT, TRY USING A SINGLE WEAVER. THICK, WHITE CROCHET TWINE CAN ALSO BE USED IN PLACE OF THE CANE 'WEAVER'. THIS GIVES A FINE FINISH REMINISCENT OF THE LLOYD LOOM STYLE OF WHITE-PAINTED WICKERWORK. A FURTHER VARIATION IS TO WEAVE WITH SILVER BEADING WIRE IN PLACE OF CANE. WITH THIS METHOD, YOU CAN MAKE A DECORATIVE SILVER BASKET FOR BREAD ROLLS.

Fig 11.8 Weaving the border.

000 cane. Thread these into one of the stake holes. Use a cocktail stick to help the cane through.

2 Carefully bend the cane to form a

BELOW LEFT: *Fig 11.9 Weaving the basket lid.*

BELOW RIGHT: *Fig 11.10 Attaching handles to the basket.*

handle and thread the other ends into the next stake hole.

3 Fit a second handle opposite the first.

4 Adjust the handles to size.

Lid

1 Make the lid in the same way as the base, but with no upsett. Pair round until the lid fits the basket top.

2 Soak the lid and work the border.

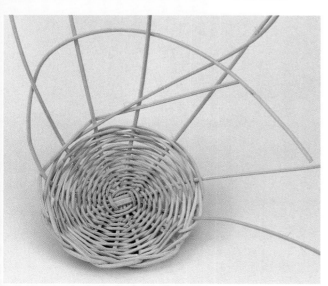

TECHNIQUE
Weaving

Weaving is very straightforward so long as you follow a few simple guidelines. For miniature purposes, a child's loom is ideal. Children's 'toy' weaving looms often turn up in charity shops. If there are no instructions included don't be put off; the loom isn't difficult to **span** (thread up). Failing that, get one from the craft department of a large toy store or from a craft catalogue.

'Beading looms', available from mail-order bead and craft suppliers, are narrow, but have **warp thread** slots close together, which is ideal. Look at the distance between the 'threading-up' slots on either end of the loom or the closeness of the holes or slots in the **heddle**. A closer warp will result in a finer weave which is more suitable for miniature work.

PROJECT
Woven Rag Rug

A rag rug is an excellent introduction to weaving, particularly miniature weaving, because the result isn't designed to be fine or delicate. Another advantage is that the rag rugs are very quick to make. Span the loom with fine twine. (Crochet cotton is ideal for rag rugs. Odd balls are generally available in charity shops.) The weft threads are made from strips of fabric. Lightweight cotton print works best.

Materials

- Child's weaving loom
- Thin crochet cotton
- Lightweight cotton fabrics, in two colours

METHOD

Preparation

1. Span (thread) the loom with crochet cotton to the required width. My mat measured 2¾in (70mm). Be sure to incorporate the heddle in the threading.

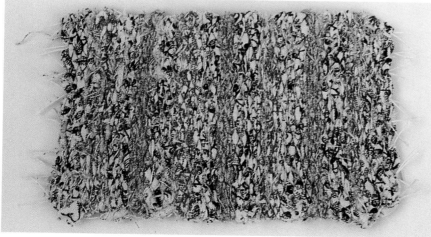

WOVEN RAG RUG.

Fig 11.11 Spanned weaving loom.

RUG WEAVING

◆ Plan the pattern of the rug before you begin weaving.

◆ Choose toning or contrasting fabric for the strips.

◆ Cut the strips neatly with scissors. If you tear along the grain, the frayed edges can make the rug look messy.

◆ The easiest way to cut the strips is to fold the fabric in half several times and snip off strips at the folded end.

◆ As you weave, leave the strip ends dangling. These will be sewn in when the rug is finished.

◆ Tidy the finished rug by snipping off some of the stray threads.

2 Cut about half a dozen ¼in x 3ft (6mm x 1m) strips from your chosen fabrics.

Weaving

1 Thread the end of one strip through the shuttle, pull the heddle up to part the threads and 'throw' the

shuttle through them. Catch the shuttle on the other side.

2 Use the heddle to 'bang' down the first weft thread against the base of the loom.

3 Pull the heddle up and throw the shuttle back through the threads. Neaten the turn, which will make the

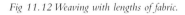

Fig 11.12 Weaving with lengths of fabric.

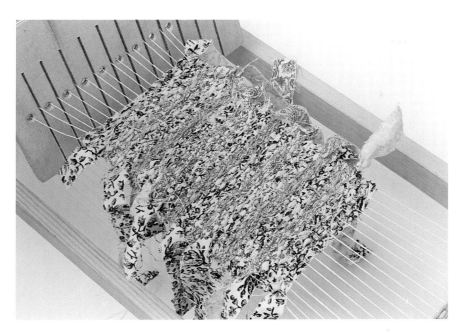

Fig 11.13 The completed length of rug.

selvage, and bang the second weft thread down.

4 Continue to the end of the strip. Be sure to bang the weft threads well down to achieve a close weave.

5 Repeat the weaving process with a second strip in a different colour.

6 Carry on weaving until your rug is long enough. Mine measures 4in (102mm).

7 Sew the loose fabric ends into the back of the weave with a large darning needle.

Fringe

1 Cut the rug loose from the warp threads.

2 Knot the warp threads tightly against the weave to secure the weft threads and stop them unravelling.

3 Trim the warp threads at each end of the rug to make the fringe.

TECHNIQUE
Cross Stitch

Cross stitch work never goes out of fashion. It is one of the simplest forms of decorative needlework. Thread is stitched through holes in a loosely woven fabric. The pattern is systematically followed by counting the holes in the fabric. All crafts can be addictive, but cross stitch is particularly so. Try it once and you're hooked.

All fabrics sold for cross stitch have a regular weave. They are classified by the number of holes per inch (hpi). The hpi determines the size of the finished design: the higher the hpi, the smaller the scale of the design. Miniature work is generally classified as 18hpi or less. The scale you work in will depend mostly on your eyesight, because you'll need to see the holes to sew through them. Specialist suppliers stock scale embroidery canvas and silk gauze. Silk gauze is available at 48hpi, 60hpi, and even 84hpi. These tiny scales are best left to the experts.

Tent stitch, which is half a cross stitch, is the best stitch for miniature work. It's less bulky than a full cross stitch and has the advantage of being

CROSS STITCH

◆ Work in a good light, preferably daylight. Magnifying spectacles, available from chemists, are invaluable for preventing eyestrain.

◆ You can design your own cross stitch charts by colouring in squares on fine graph paper to make up a picture.

◆ To save buying several skeins of embroidery silk, look for the multicoloured skeins made up of about three shades of the same colour. Simply snip the skein into its different shades.

◆ Use two threads of ordinary embroidery silk, or one strand for very fine work.

◆ Thread needles with all the required colours before you begin to sew.

◆ Keep your working thread to a manageable length. It saves time in the end because a long thread always becomes knotted and grubby and wears thin from friction on the canvas.

◆ It's not necessary to knot threads.

◆ To stop unused threads dangling and knotting up, catch their needles into the side or back of the surplus fabric to keep them out of the way.

◆ Each stitch should slope the same way; always work in the same direction.

◆ Try to keep your stitches evenly tensioned; neither too loose nor too tight.

continued on page 131

quicker to sew. The picture is built up working from a chart marked with colours (or numbers/symbols which correspond to colours). Each square on the chart represents one stitch (not one hole). Begin sewing where the chart suggests; this could be in one of the corners or in the centre. To give a neat, even appearance, all the stitches must be worked in the same direction. For right-handers, it is easier to stitch from left to right then back from right to left. Left-handers may find it more comfortable to reverse the pattern and begin in the top left-hand corner. Stitch from right to left then back from left to right. The design will look the same, but the tent stitch will slope the other way.

PROJECT

Cross Stitch Rose Cushion

A cross stitch cushion is an excellent project for a beginner because, if the threads on the back become bulky, they can easily be hidden inside the cushion. If they're really bulky, you may not even need to use stuffing! I used 25hpi for this project, making a cushion measuring 1⅜in (33mm) square. You can use a larger or smaller gauge fabric if you prefer. The size of the canvas doesn't have to be precise, but very small snippets of canvas can be fiddly to work with.

METHOD

Stitching

❶ Thread the needles with 12in (300mm) lengths of each colour thread.

❷ Begin in the centre of the canvas and work to the right. Refer to the chart given in Fig 11.14 to find out which colour thread to work with. Bring the needle out in the central hole. (Choose any hole to be the central hole so long as there's enough surrounding fabric to accommodate the pattern easily.)

❸ Thread the needle down through the hole one row above and to the right of the central hole. This is your first stitch, and should slope to the right.

❹ Bring the needle out through the fabric again in the hole adjacent to the

CROSS STITCH ROSE CUSHION.

Materials

◆ Embroidery fabric, 25hpi: 5in (127mm) square

◆ Embroidery silks: brown, pale green, dark green, dark pink, mid-pink, pale pink, gold and yellow

◆ Fine sewing needles x 8

◆ Kapok or cotton wool

◆ Snippet of silk backing fabric (to tone with embroidery silks)

◆ Soutache (plain trim), ¼yd (¼m) (to tone with embroidery silks)

◆ Sewing thread, to match soutache

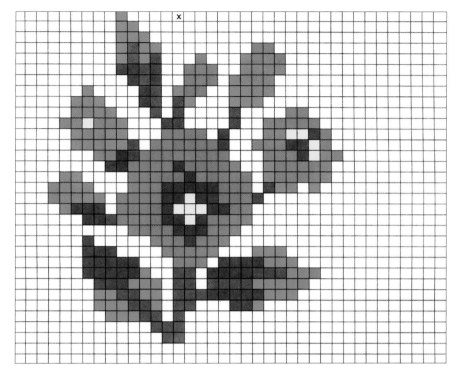

Fig 11.14 Stitch chart for rose design.

continued from page 130

- Resist the temptation to skip about the pattern. Work the pattern systematically row by row.
- As you complete each row, cross it off the chart.
- For beginners, it is best to avoid patterns of people and animals and stick to flowers or foliage – these designs accommodate some miss-stitching more convincingly.
- If you are working on fabric canvas you can stitch in the background or not as you wish, but bear in mind that stitching in the background represents a lot more work.
- If you are working on gauze, which looks like fine plastic mesh, the whole area needs to be stitched in so that the gauze is no longer visible.
- Experts say a fine piece of embroidery should be as neat on the back as it is on the front. Well, mine certainly isn't.

central hole and repeat step 3. Carry on to the end of the row, changing thread colour as the chart indicates.

5 At the end of the row work back to the left, stitching the row above, ensuring that the stitch continues to slope to the right.

Fig 11.15 Stitching the pattern, working up from the centre.

KEY TO CROSS STITCH CUSHION

- RED
- MID RED
- DARK RED
- YELLOW
- LIGHT GREEN
- MID-GREEN
- DARK GREEN

Fig 11.16 The top half of the pattern completed.

Fig 11.17 The pattern completed.

Fig 11.18 Stitching into a cushion.

FURTHER APPLICATIONS

WORKED CROSS STITCH CAN BE USED LIKE ANY OTHER DECORATIVE TEXTILE. CROSS STITCH DESIGNS CAN MAKE ATTRACTIVE SEAT COVERS, TAPESTRY BAGS AND EVEN TINY SLIPPERS. IT CAN ALSO BE DISPLAYED AS ART; MOUNTED AS A WALL HANGING OR FRAMED AS A PICTURE.

6 Continue working rows backwards and forwards until you come to the top of the chart.

7 Begin again at the centre and work to the left. Continue working rows backwards and forwards until the pattern is complete.

8 You can either stitch the remaining canvas with a background colour such as cream, or leave it unstitched as I have.

Making up

1 Trim the canvas to 1in (25mm) all round the pattern.

2 Fold and pin the excess fabric onto the wrong side so that the sides are all the same length and the pattern is centred in the square.

3 Fold and pin a square of silk fabric to the same dimensions.

4 Line up the silk backing fabric, right-side out, with the embroidered

fabric square, right-side up, and pin together.

5 Slip stitch three of the seams with tiny stitches.

6 Stuff lightly with kapok or cotton wool.

7 Turn in the remaining seam neatly and close up the cushion with slip stitch.

Trim

1 Stitch the edges of the soutache together with matching thread to make a length of tiny piping trim.

2 Using matching thread, stitch the piping round the seams to disguise the slip stitches. Make a small decorative loop at each corner if you like the effect (see photo of finished piece).

3 Tuck the end of the trim inside the cushion to secure a neat finish.

CHAPTER TWELVE

Objets
d'Art

Objets d'Art

Objets d'art, such as ornaments, paintings and small decorative furnishings, are a wonderful way to bring a miniature room setting to life. Only so much furniture can be fitted into a room, but often ornaments can continue to be added. They tell us something about the inhabitants as well as giving a sense of period. For example, to create the feeling of high Victoriana which was in style during the latter half of the nineteenth century, cover every surface with ornaments and doilies.

Glass gluing technique

Glass glue will not cure under electric lighting; it will still cure outside on a cloudy day, but may take several minutes. This won't be a problem if the components don't need to be supported while they dry.

1. As with other glues, the surfaces to be glued must be clean and dry. Wash the glass components in soapy water and dry them thoroughly with a lint-free cloth. (Scrub old glass buttons with an old toothbrush if necessary.)
2. Prepare a level work surface in full sunlight, but begin work with the components in full shade. A shoebox with one side cut away gives all-round shade.
3. Place a dot of glass glue onto one of the surfaces, then immediately place the next glass component onto the glue.
4. If it doesn't balance, hold it in place with one hand as you remove the shoebox with the other.
5. The glass glue will cure as soon as the sunrays hit the glass. Gently remove your finger and leave the project undisturbed for a few minutes.

The scope for making ornaments is only limited by your imagination. The ones included here are just examples of specific techniques which you can adopt and adapt as you require. Inspiration is all around. You may see something you'd like to make in a book, on television or in someone's house.

TECHNIQUE
Gluing Glass

DIY glassware is one of my most surprising (and pleasing) discoveries. Impressive results can be easily achieved with nothing more than a few glass buttons and glass glue. Glass glue is a specialist glue made from hydroxypropyl methacrylate. It is readily available in small tubes from DIY and stationery stores and it really does glue glass. It dries within a few seconds when exposed to ultraviolet light (a component of sunlight) so when working with glass glue, it's best to work outside on a sunny day. You will find your project progresses much quicker this way.

Attractive glassware can be made from glass buttons, but of course you can incorporate any tiny glass or crystal ornament or bead into your project. I made an impressive table centrepiece simply by gluing together three glass fish beads and a large glass button.

PROJECT
Crystal Fruit Bowl

New glass buttons aren't widely available nowadays, but they can often be picked up in charity shops, flea markets and antique fairs. Odd glass buttons are still very cheap, even in antique shops, because they are of little use to anyone. Small bags of odd buttons are sometimes sold off cheaply.

Most glass buttons can be used to good
effect, so buy them up when you see
them. Shank buttons (with projecting
shank thread holes) make good bases or
lids. Look out for coloured and gilded
buttons, which make particularly
attractive glassware.

Once you have a collection of glass
buttons, add a few crystal beads and
rhinestones and you can make a vast
array of glassware and crystalware.
Experiment with different arrange-
ments to get the best effects before
gluing the components together. Try
cake stands, ashtrays, trinket dishes,
bonbon jars, fruit bowls and dessert
dishes. In one charity shop button box
I managed to find six matching 'bowl'
buttons and six matching 'base' buttons
so that I could make a set of six sundae
glasses – this hardly ever happens.

METHOD

1 Wash the buttons and beads in
soapy water and dry thoroughly.
2 Working in the shade, place the
large button on a level working surface,
face down. Place a dot of glass glue
between the thread holes.
3 Immediately position the thread

CRYSTAL FRUIT BOWL.

Materials

- Large glass button
- Medium glass button
- Crystal bead
- Glass glue

Fig 12.1 The component glass buttons and bead.

GLASS BUTTON GLUING

◆ Charity shop buttons are invariably dusty. Always wash glass buttons before gluing them. Not only will this give a clean surface for gluing, it also ensures that the finished project sparkles as it should.

◆ For the best results, the buttons and beads must sit squarely on top of each other. The easiest way to balance the buttons squarely is to position yourself so that you can look down onto the top of the components and line up the thread holes by eye.

◆ If you want to glue small components, such as beads or rhinestones, it can be tricky to balance a large button on a tiny bead. Glue the bead onto the button, then glue the next bead or button on top.

◆ Nowadays glass buttons have largely been replaced by glass-look plastic ones. Plastic buttons can also make reasonable glassware, but should be glued with superglue.

TRANSFER EMULSION

◆ If your transfer tears as you remove the backing, you have applied too few coats of emulsion.

◆ If the finished picture is thick and cloudy, you have applied too many coats of emulsion.

◆ Transfers can be glued onto wood, paper and pottery surfaces.

◆ As a water-based varnish, transfer emulsion can be used for decoupage (decorating objects with paper clippings). It can also be tinted with acrylic paint to give an antique finish.

Fig 12.2 Gluing the components together.

VARIATIONS

RHINESTONES (THE TYPE WITHOUT SILVERED BACKING IS BEST) IN VARIOUS SIZES CAN BE COMBINED WITH CRYSTAL BEADS TO MAKE A SELECTION OF ATTRACTIVE SCENT BOTTLES.

hole of the crystal bead on top of the glue and allow to cure for a few minutes in sunlight.

④ Shade the project again and place a dot of glass glue over the crystal bead's thread hole.

⑤ Immediately position the small button, face up, over the bead.

⑥ Expose to sunlight and leave undisturbed for a few minutes, to cure.

TECHNIQUE

Making Transfers

Water-based transfer emulsion is a versatile medium and extremely useful to the miniaturist. It's sold under various brand names, including Decal-it, Lift off and Super Sealer. Transfer emulsion can turn any picture or catalogue clipping into a custom-made transfer. Transfer emulsion also doubles as a water-based varnish. It can be used to give paper, wood or plastic a sheen, and can also be used as a glue.

PROJECT

Oil Painting

One very effective way of adding atmosphere to a room setting is to hang pictures. Miniaturists have been framing small catalogue clippings as prints for decades, but miniature oil paintings look even more effective. Needless to say, painting miniatures in oils takes great skill. Here is my method which gives impressive results in minutes … with no artistic ability required! Simply mount the picture transfer onto fabric that resembles fine canvas: calico has a visible weave that looks similar to artists' canvas.

Picture frames can be easily made up from picture frame moulding (available from dolls' house shops or mail order). As with full-size picture frames, some have rebates on the back into which the painting is fitted. Basic frames can be decorated to complement any period. To make a more elaborate frame, I glued on fennel and poppy seeds before finishing with gold spray paint and a proprietary antiquing gel. Oil paintings can be hung from a picture rail, from twine or fine chain attached to the back of the painting. For a more modern look, simply attach the picture to the wall with a wax

OIL PAINTINGS.

fixing medium such as Gripwax. This does a similar job to Blu-tack, but is less obtrusive and so is ideal for fixing miniatures in place.

METHOD

Making the transfer

1 Cut out the picture, leaving a 1in (25mm) border all round. Tape it to a piece of scrap paper such as newspaper.

2 Coat the entire picture clipping with a thin coat of transfer emulsion.

3 Allow the first coat to dry for a couple of minutes, then apply a second

Materials

◆ Picture clipping
◆ Transfer emulsion
◆ Fine-weave calico
◆ Picture frame moulding
◆ Spray paint: gold (optional)
◆ Decorative seeds, e.g. fennel and poppy (optional)
◆ Wood stain
◆ French polish
◆ Superglue
◆ Wood glue

Fig 12.3 Coating the clippings with transfer emulsion.

Transfers technique

1 Cut out the clipping, leaving a 1in (25mm) margin all round. Tape the clipping to a piece of scrap paper.

2 Cover the entire clipping with a thin coat of transfer emulsion, overlapping the edges of the picture. Leave to dry for 2–3 minutes.

3 Paint on a second coat in the opposite direction, keeping the coating thin and even.

4 Apply four or five more coats, alternating the direction of application, allowing each to dry. (Don't worry if the picture buckles a little at this stage.) Stop applying emulsion when the picture begins to fog.

5 Leave the clipping to cure for about an hour.

6 Soak the picture in warm water for about 15 minutes until it is completely saturated.

7 Lay the clipping face down on scrap paper and gently rub off the paper backing with your finger. Apply more water if needed. The finished transfer should be semi-transparent. If not, re-soak. Be sure to remove all the backing paper before mounting the transfer.

8 Mount the transfer using the transfer emulsion as glue.

KNOW-HOW

OIL PAINTING

◆ Use any picture from a magazine or catalogue, printed on glossy or matt paper.

◆ Select a picture that has been photographed straight-on. If the original is distorted, no matter how attractive it is, the result will be disappointing.

◆ To give a realistic effect, stretch the mounted canvas tautly in the frame, but be careful not to tear the transferred picture.

◆ A mitre block takes the guesswork out of cutting accurate angles when making up a picture frame.

◆ For a professional finish to the picture frame, the opposing sides must be cut to the same length. (But if you trim off too much to even the lengths, you will finish up with a very tiny frame.)

continued on page 139

coat in the opposite direction, keeping the coating even.

④ Apply four or five more coats, alternating the direction of application, and allowing to dry between coats. Stop if the picture begins to fog.

⑤ Set the picture aside to cure for about 1 hour.

⑥ Soak the picture in warm water for

Fig 12.4 Soaking and removing the backing.

about 15 minutes, until it is completely saturated.

⑦ Lay the picture face down on a piece of scrap paper and gently rub off the paper backing with your finger.

Fig 12.5 Mounting the transfers on calico.

Fig 12.6 Staining and painting the frames.

continued from page 138

- ◆ Measure the required length for the picture frame and mark this on the longer length of the picture frame moulding.
- ◆ Don't use too much pressure when sawing mouldings. They are made of softwood and will easily splinter or snap.
- ◆ Wood glue is best for picture frames which need to be ridged. (The flexible bond of tacky glue results in a wobbly frame.)
- ◆ Butt the drying frame into a 'jig' to ensure that it doesn't warp. A jig is simply a device to hold your project in place while it dries. The simplest jig is a box or household tray with straight, right angle corners.
- ◆ Remember that wood stain cannot penetrate glue. It's often easier to stain or paint the frame moulding before cutting and gluing.
- ◆ Wood frames also look attractive when gilded with gold spray paint or gold leaf.

Re-soak if necessary. Be sure to remove all the backing paper.

8 Pat the picture dry with kitchen paper.

Mounting the picture

1 Choose a smooth section of calico with no lumps in the weave. Spread some of the transfer emulsion onto the back of the picture. Press it firmly onto the calico and gently smooth on. Set aside to dry.

Making the frame

1 Use a mitre block and junior hacksaw to make up a picture frame from picture frame moulding. Measure the required length of moulding. Before cutting, double-check that the moulding is the correct way round in the mitre block and that the cut is the appropriate right- or left-sloping cut.

2 Glue the frame together with wood glue. Set aside to dry, but ensure that the frame dries square by butting it into a simple jig.

3 Stain the frame with wood stain and apply a few coats of french polish.

Gilded frame

1 Decorate the frame, if you like the effect, by gluing on suitable seeds or spices with superglue.

2 Spray with a couple of coats of gold paint.

3 Distress by rubbing on a little antiquing gel.

Framing the picture

1 Spread some glue onto the back of the frame and place it over the picture.

2 Gently stretch and trim the picture to fit squarely inside the frame.

3 When the glue is dry, trim any excess fabric from around the frame with a craft knife.

FURTHER APPLICATIONS

COAT TARTAN PRINT WITH A COAT OF TRANSFER EMULSION TO MAKE A WATERPROOF PICNIC GROUNDSHEET. COAT SMALL-PATTERNED PAPER WITH A COAT OF TRANSFER EMULSION TO MAKE DRAWER- AND SHELF-LINING PAPER.

KNOW-HOW

INSTALLING ELECTRICS

◆ You can use insulated wire if you prefer this method to copper tape.

◆ Since the copper tape needs to be concealed, install the electrics *before* wallpapering.

◆ Make a sketch or take a snapshot of the finished circuit layout *before* you decorate so that you can see at a glance where the circuits run once the decorations are in place.

◆ Don't wallpaper over uninsulated copper tape with wallpaper paste. The water and fungicide content of the paste can cause the copper to oxidize and may turn your wallpaper green! Spray or paint a lacquer suitable for use on metal, such as car spray lacquer, over the tape to prevent this.

◆ It is a good idea to lay most of the copper tape on the floors: false floors can then be laid over the top. This will give easy access to most of the circuit, which is useful if you want to add another electrical connection and need to run extra tape from the main circuit.

◆ Since the copper tape needs to form an unbroken electrical circuit, remember to connect each 'break' in the tape with specialist metal 'connecting pins' (tiny eyelets available from miniature lighting suppliers).

◆ Keep testing your circuit as you lay it by checking that it lights a wired bulb. This way you will know instantly if you have broken the connection.

continued on page 141

TECHNIQUE
Electrifying Lamps

A book on dolls' house know-how wouldn't be complete without a lighting project. If you choose not to electrify your dolls' house, you'll wish you had when you've completed it. Illumination adds immeasurably to any dolls' house. Considering the minimal expense, it's well worth the extra effort. If you have a large dolls' house, it can become very expensive to buy several lights for each room. It's much more economical and far more fun to make your own. I love making dolls' house lighting. The results are always unique and you can tailor your lamp to fit your chosen period.

Lighting looks impressive and really is easy to achieve even if you are a complete beginner. If you can use Sellotape, you can electrify a dolls' house. And once the circuit is installed, think of all the fun you can have making many beautiful miniature lamps. Several helpful books and pamphlets on the subject are available (see Bibliography, page 144). If you buy an electrifying kit, this will include detailed instructions. Your local dolls' house shop will be happy to advise on the basic technique, which uses copper tape laid in a double strip, throughout the house. Wired light bulbs are connected to the strip, which is then connected to a transformer that plugs into your household electrical socket. The transformer reduces the 240 volts down to a mere 12 volts, which is similar to a battery and safe even for children.

PROJECT
Edgar Brandt Lamp

Copies of this 1920s designer lamp by Edgar Brandt are still on sale today. Transparent Fimo is ideal for making this type of delicate Edwardian glass lampshade. They take very little effort to make and every one is unique. The cobra (snake) decoration is fun to make from Milliput. When you're modelling, it's always helpful to work from a picture. This takes away much of the guesswork because copying an image is always easier than trying to conjure one up in your head.

I achieved the snakeskin effect by pressing a snippet of tulle over the finished model. You will find modelling the cobra easier if you work with Milliput that is three-quarters hardened. Just to encourage you, I think Milliput is easier to model than Fimo.

EDGAR BRANDT LAMP.

FAR LEFT: *Fig 12.7 Assembling the lamp structure.*

LEFT: *Fig 12.8 Fitting the Fimo shade.*

METHOD

The base

1. Cut a length of aluminium tube to measure 1⅝in (41mm). Ensure that both ends are clear of metal burrs (rough edges) and that they are not squashed.

2. Drill the centre out of the small decorative button with a ¹⁄₁₆in (2mm) drill bit.

3. Place one end of the aluminium tube in the centre of the button and press a pea-sized ball of Milliput round it, shaping the Milliput to the tube. Ensure that the tube hole remains unblocked. Set aside to harden.

4. Thread the small wooden bead, followed by the lice bead, onto the top of the aluminium tube. (You may need to enlarge the thread hole slightly with a drill bit.)

5. Thread the eyelet, flat-side down, on top of the bead.

6. Glue both beads and eyelet in place, level with the top of the tube, with superglue.

7. Spray the stand with a couple of coats of gold spray paint.

The shade

1. Cut one ¼in (6mm) square block and two ⅛in (3mm) square blocks of transparent polymer clay.

2. Mix a scraping of orange polymer clay into one of the ⅛in (3mm) blocks.

3. Mix a scraping of purple polymer clay into the other ⅛in (3mm) block.

4. Blend a peppercorn of yellow into the remaining ¼in (6mm) block.

5. Mix a couple of specks of purple

Materials

- ³⁄₃₂in (2mm) brass or aluminium tubing
- Small wooden bead
- Small wooden 'lice' bead
- Small metal eyelet
- Polymer clay: transparent, orange, yellow and purple
- Milliput: superfine white
- Snippet of tulle
- Spray paint: gold
- Dressmakers' pin
- Small decorative button
- Superglue
- 12 volt bulb with fine wires

continued from page 140

- Always ensure that the voltage of your bulbs matches that of your transformer. The voltage generally used by adult miniaturists is 12 volts.

- You can power a maximum of nine 12 volt bulbs simultaneously from one 12 volt transformer. If this is not enough for your dolls' house, you can remedy this by laying a separately switched circuit on each floor. However, this means that not all the floors can be illuminated at once.

LAMP MAKING

◆ Try to keep superglue off bulb wire; it can melt the plastic coating and cause an electrical short.

◆ Keep access for the bulb wires (usually metal tubing) free from glue and modelling material.

into the yellow block so that they are visible as swirls.

6 Press the three blocks together with the yellow in the centre. Roll and squash it gently until an attractive pattern results. Don't overwork the ball – the marbling is easily lost.

7 Shape the ball into a cone. Press a modelling tool (I used the end of a ballpoint pen) into the wide end of the cone and work out a hollow centre.

8 Once you have a rough hollow cone shape, set it aside to cool and firm up.

9 Thin out the sides to a uniform thickness, which should be thin enough for the light to show through. Trim the cone to ¾in (19mm) in height.

10 Press the pen end into the base of the cone to cut out a hole that will fit over the eyelet on the lamp stand. (Don't make this too tight a fit because polymer clay shrinks very slightly during hardening and the lampshade might split if you force it onto the eyelet.)

11 Harden the shade in a cool oven, 100°C (200°F), for 10 minutes.

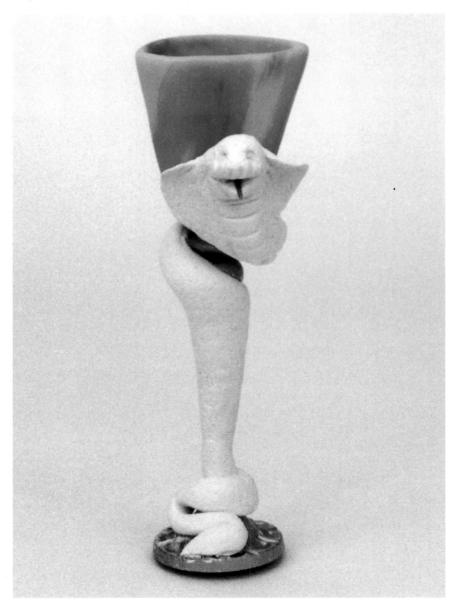

Fig 12.9 Fixing on the snake decoration.

12 Once cool, glue the shade to the stand with superglue.

Snake decoration

1 Mix up a marble-sized ball of superfine Milliput. Set this aside to harden for about one hour, but no longer.

2 Completely cover the aluminium stem of the lamp with a thin layer of Milliput, and smooth this down so that the layer gradually thickens towards the top where the cobra's body will be. Don't cover the bead at the top.

3 Roll a thin, tapering snake tail from Milliput. Blend the thicker end of the tail to the end of the Milliput-covered stem. Smooth the join so that the tail runs into the body fluidly.

4 Curl and twist the tail round the base once and coil it up at the front (see Fig 12.9).

5 Roll a slightly thicker sausage shape for the head and upper body of the cobra. Model the top jaw of the cobra's head at one end. Pinch out the 'hood' at each side of the head and neck, then thin and refine the shape of the hood.

6 From a thin section of Milliput, model the cobra's lower jaw. Stick this under the upper jaw, blending in the join.

7 Centre the finished head on the clay lampshade, directly above the coiled tail and press into place. Twine the attached body top round the lampshade once and blend the end into the tail section on the lamp stand. The join should encircle the round bead and lice bead. If Milliput has smeared over them, scrape it off with a craft knife.

8 Blend and smooth all the joins well so that the snake body flows smoothly.

9 Mark out the two vertical lines to outline the cobra's underbelly with the blunt side of a craft knife. Press on horizontal lines down this section (see Fig 12.9).

10 Press a single layer of tulle over the

Fig 12.10 Fitting the wired bulb.

entire snake, except for the lined underbelly.

11 Mark eyes on each side of the head with the head of a dressmakers' pin.

12 Press the point of the pin onto the cobra's nose to mark two nostrils.

13 Snip off the point of the pin with power scissors and press this into the open mouth of the hissing cobra to make the tongue.

14 Ensure that the cobra's head is in the correct position before setting the model aside to harden completely.

15 Once hardened, carefully paint the entire snake gold (avoiding the lampshade).

Fitting the bulb

1 Lightly twist the bulb wires together and thread them through the centre of the aluminium tube at the centre of the lamp.

2 Gently pull the bulb into position so that it sits on top of the tube.

3 Connect the wires to your dolls' house electrical circuit.

> **VARIATIONS**
>
> A VARIETY OF ART NOUVEAU-STYLE GLASS LAMP SHADES CAN BE MADE USING TRANSPARENT POLYMER CLAY. LOOK IN ANTIQUE BOOKS FOR PICTURES OF 'DAUM' LAMPS TO COPY. THE BASES ARE USUALLY NATURALISTIC DESIGNS SUCH AS TREE TRUNKS.

Glossary of British and American Terms

British	American	British	American
Blu-tack	Fun-tak	French polish	Furniture polish
Ceiling rose	Medallion	Fridge	Refrigerator
Charity shop	Thrift shop	Haberdashery	Notions
Chemist	Drugstore	Piping bag	Pastry bag
Cocktail stick	Round tooth-pick	Plait	Braid
Cornice	Crown molding	Pelmet	Cornice
Cotton bud	Q-tip	Polyfilla	Spackle
Dado	Wainscoting	Skirting	Baseboard
Draughtboard	Checkerboard	Stationers	Stationery store
Duster	Dust cloth	Stockist	Retailer
Elastic band	Rubber band	Tack (stitch)	Baste
Embroidery silk	DMS floss	Transfer	Decal
Emulsion	Latex	White spirit	Mineral spirit

Bibliography

Abbey Fine Arts, *Victoriana,* Murray Group of Companies, London, 1970

Curtis, T, *The Lyle Official Antiques Review* (various)

Everleigh, D J, *Firegrates and Kitchen Ranges,* Shire Publications Ltd, Buckinghamshire, 1983

Gilliatt, M, *Period Decorating,* Conran Octopus Ltd, London, 1990

Hodges, F, *Period Pastimes; A Practical Guide to Four Centuries of Decorative Crafts,* Weidenfeld & Nicolson, New York, 1989

Innes, J, *Scandinavian Painted Decor,* Cassell, London, 1990

Manwaring, K, *How to Electrify a Dollshouse Using Copper Tape (9th edition),* pamphlet available from Wood'n'Wool Miniatures (see Suppliers, page 146)

Maynard, B, *Basketry in Easy Steps,* Macmillan Publishing Company Inc., New York, 1977

Millers Antique Price Guides (various)

Seymour, J, *Forgotten Household Crafts,* Guild Publishing, London, 1987

Thornton, P, *Authentic Decor; The Domestic Interior 1620–1920,* Weidenfeld & Nicolson, London, 1984

Metric Conversion Table

Inches to millimetres and centimetres

in	mm	cm
⅛	3	0.3
¼	6	0.6
⅜	10	1.0
½	13	1.3
⅝	16	1.6
¾	19	1.9
⅞	22	2.2
1	25	2.5
1¼	32	3.2
1½	38	3.8
1¾	44	4.4
2	51	5.1
2½	64	6.4
3	76	7.6
3½	89	8.9
4	102	10.2
4½	114	11.4
5	127	12.7
6	152	15.2
7	178	17.8
8	203	20.3

in	cm
9	22.9
10	25.4
11	27.9
12	30.5
13	33.0
14	35.6
15	38.1
16	40.6
17	43.2
18	45.7
19	48.3
20	50.8
21	53.3
22	55.9
23	58.4
24	61.0
25	63.5
26	66.0
27	68.6
28	71.1
29	73.7

in	cm
30	76.2
31	78.7
32	81.3
33	83.8
34	86.4
35	88.9
36	91.4
37	94.0
38	96.5
39	99.1
40	101.6
41	104.1
42	106.7
43	109.2
44	111.8
45	114.3
46	116.8
47	119.4
48	121.9
49	124.5
50	127.0

Suppliers

UNITED KINGDOM

Mail order miniature and hobby suppliers

Hobby's Annual
Knight's Hill Square, London, SE27
0HH
Tel: 0181 7614244

Furniture sets

Hobbies (Dereham) Ltd
34–36 Swaffham Rd, Dereham,
Norfolk, NR19 2QZ
Tel: 01362 692985

Electrics

Wood 'n' Wool Electrics
Unit 1 Old Co-op Yard, Kellet Rd,
Carnforth, Lancashire, LA 5 9LR
Tel: 01524 720277
<K.J.Manwaring@mcmail.com>

Didiments
18 Kings Drive, Carnforth, Lancashire
LA5 9AG
Tel: 01524 736609

Wood

Wood Supplies
94 Colliers Water Lane, Thornton
Heath, Surrey CR7 7LB
Tel: 0181 6891865

Mouldings

Borcraft Miniatures
Robin Business Centre, Leeds Rd,
Greengates, Bradford,
West Yorkshire BD10 9TE
Tel: 01274 622577
<enquiries@borcraft–miniature.co.uk>

Beads and findings

Kaleidoscope Crafts
(Beads and findings)
3 Grove Park, Brislington,
Bristol BS4 3LG
Fax: 0117 972 3739

Creative Beadcraft Ltd
Denmark Works, Sheepcote Dell Rd,
Beamond End, Near Amersham,
Buckinghamshire HP7 0RX
Tel: 01494 715606

Tee Pee Crafts
28 Holborn Drive, Mackworth, Derby
DE22 4DX
Tel: 01332 332772

Haberdashery

The Dollshouse Draper
PO Box 128, Lightcliffe, Halifax, West
Yorkshire HX3 8RN
Tel: 01422 201 275

Leather

Ordanna Supplies (Glove leather)
6 Sheppards Rise, Brinkworth,
Wiltshire SN15 5BE
Tel: 01666 510677

Miniature cane

Ann Underwood Miniatures
20 Park Lane, Glemsford, Sudbury,
Suffolk CO10 7QQ
Tel: 01787 281372

Craft supplies

Panduro Hobby
Transport Ave, Brentford, Middlesex
TW8 8BR
Tel: 0181 8476161

Fred Aldous Ltd
37 Lever St, Manchester M60 1UX
Tel: 0161 2362477

UNITED STATES

With thanks to the on-line miniature
newsgroup Tiny
Talk<http://www.inet-
serv.com/~tinytalk/index.html>

Mail order miniature and hobby suppliers

Hobby Builders Supply
PO Box 921012, Norcross, GA
Tel: 30092-7012

Dee's Delights
(Including K & S Metal)
3150 State Line Rd
North Bend, OH 45052
Tel: 513-353-3390
email <dees@one.net>

Electrics

(Contact for nearest supplier)
Cir-Kit Concepts, Inc.
407 14th St NW
Rochester, MN 55901
Tel: 507-288-0860

Wood and mouldings

(Contact for nearest supplier)
Houseworks
2388 Pleasantdale Rd
Atlanta, GA 30340
Tel: 1-770-448-6596

Beads

Enterprise Art
2860 Roosevelt Blvd
Clearwater, FL 33770
Tel: 1-800-366-2218
email <custserv@enterpriseart.com>
<http://www.enterpriseart.com>

Jewelry findings

JAF Miniatures
RR # 3
Osceola, MO 64776
Tel: 417-646-8642

Rings & Things
PO Box 450
Spokane, WA 99210-0450
Fax: 509-838-2602
Tel: 509-624-8565

Eastern Findings
18 W 34th St
New York, NY 10001
Tel: 212-695-6640

Notions

Sandy's Laces and Trims
Sandy Staker
7417 N. Knoxville Ave
Peoria, ILL 61614
Tel: 309-689-943
e-mail<sandys.lace.trim@juno.com>

Leather

Tandy Leather
PO Box 791
Fort Worth, TX 76101
Tel: 1800-555-3130

Craft supplies (including Milliput)

Micro Mark
340–1842 Snyder Ave
Berkley Heights, NJ 07922-1595
Tel: 1-800-225-1066
<http://www.micromark.com>

Craft King, Inc.
PO Box 90637
Lakeland, FL 33804
Tel: 1-800-769-9494

Polymer clay

American Art Clay Co. Inc.
4717 W 16 St
Indianapolis, IN 46222
Tel: 317-244-6871

Clay Factory of Escondido
750 N Citracado Pkwy nos. 22, 23
Escondido, CA 92029-1030
Tel: 619-741-3242

ABOUT THE AUTHOR

Andrea has made miniatures practically all her life. She writes regular columns for *Dolls' House World*
and *The Dolls' House Magazine* and is well known in the miniature world for her DIY projects.
This is her third book, following *Easy to Make Dolls' House Accessories* and
Making Period Dolls' House Accessories (also published by Guild of Master Craftsman Publications).
She is a member of her local writers' circle and writes full time (for the Health and Beauty industry as well
as on modelling and dolls' houses) in her jungle of a conservatory.
She lives in an Essex village with her husband, Andy.